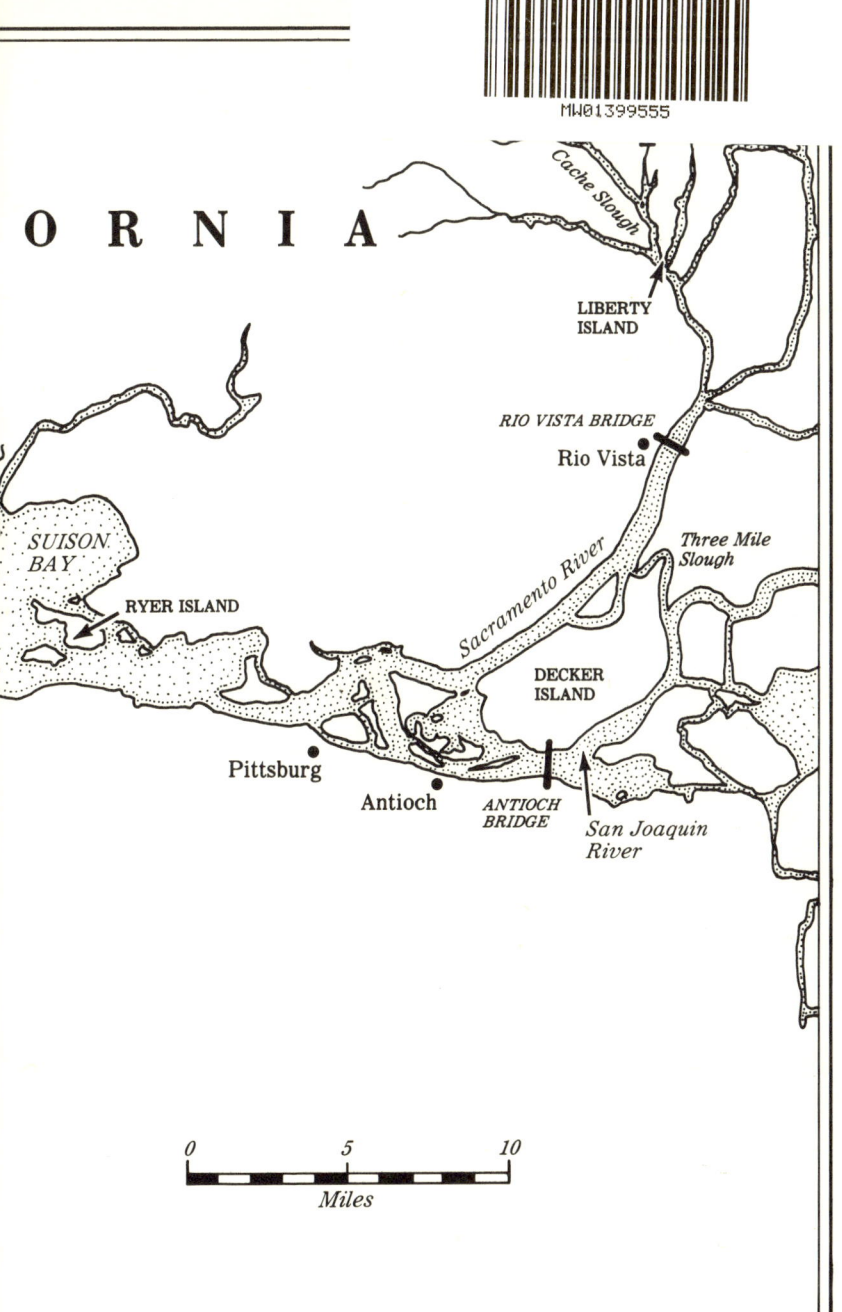

Illustration by Whitney Vosburgh

THE GREAT WHALE RESCUE

Books by Tom Tiede

CALLEY, SOLDIER OR KILLER?
COWARD
WELCOME TO WASHINGTON, MR. WITHERSPOON
YOUR MEN AT WAR

★ AN AMERICAN FOLK EPIC ★

THE GREAT WHALE RESCUE

TOM TIEDE WITH JACK FINDLETON

PHAROS BOOKS
A SCRIPPS HOWARD COMPANY
NEW YORK

Interior design: Elyse Strongin
Cover design: Nancy Eato

Copyright © 1986 by Tom Tiede and Jack Findleton

All rights reserved. No part of this book may be reproduced in any form or by any means without permission in writing from the publisher.

First published in 1986

Distributed in the United States by Ballantine Books, a division of Random House, Inc., and in Canada by Random House of Canada, Ltd.

Library of Congress Catalog Card Number: 86-60807
Pharos Books ISBN 0-88687-281-2
Ballantine Books ISBN 0-345-33912-6

Printed in the United States of America

Pharos Books
A Scrippps Howard Company
200 Park Avenue
New York, NY 10166

10 9 8 7 6 5 4 3 2 1

To Rm.

chapter one

HALFWAY THROUGH THE MONTH OF OCTOBER, IN 1985, TWO men were sitting on the bank of California's Sacramento River, waiting for favorable air. They were gathered to windsurf, that is, to ride the waves on weeny brigantines, to square, to jib, to yaw, to tack, and to run before the breeze, which, drat, was tardy that day. Usually the winds pick up on the river in the morning, particularly at a community on the water called Rio Vista. There is a bridge at that point, which frequently separates cool weather on the coast from warm weather inland, and the result is identified, for reasons lost at the origin, as the Venturi effect. Surfers say the zephyrs fairly howl at Rio Vista, and men and women with strong legs and tolerant kidneys can travel the riverway for hours on a roll, mile after mile, and pay not a farthing for petrol.

Alas, the Venturi effect can be fickle, and the windsurfers were thus stalled in a calm. Ron Wheeler sat on his board. Paul Belarde wrapped his arms around his knees. An hour passed. Another. They may have had a drab or two to while away the time. Suddenly, one of the men stood up. He pointed to an object by the shoreline. A log? No. An overturned craft? No. It was a long, black, bulging bump, shining in the autumnal sun—and swimming.

"Do you see that?" Wheeler asked.

"No."

"You do too."

The men watched as the object moved toward the bank, and, conversely, away from it, roiling the water occasionally, but quite silently, before vanishing below the surface.

Wheeler and Belarde looked at each other.

"Paul," Wheeler said.

"What?"

"We're not going to tell anyone about this, are we?"

The windsurfers had just seen the Sacramento River equivalent of the Loch Ness monster. Only this time there was no question of imagination. There was indeed a leviathan in the water. When the two men checked in with civilization that afternoon, they learned, as the world was to learn, that a humpback whale had come into the river from San Francisco Bay, where it had come previously from the Pacific Ocean. It was no fish story. The damn thing was directed inland. One of the largest animals in history, bigger by half than the dinosaur, had apparently lost its way.

The Coast Guard rushed a vessel to investigate. Private boaters set sail to witness the phenomenon, and nobody knew what in tarnation was going on. Whales live in the oceans and seas. They do not go into estuaries with the trout. One man of eighty-four years told the curious that he thought a whale may have come upriver before, in his lifetime, but that opinion was quickly shot down. Roland Lauritzen, who goes back a full ninety years in the area, always living at the edge of the water, said: "I never saw one come up before. I never heard of one coming up before, and, to tell the whole truth, my father and grandfather helped settle these parts in 1869, and they never told me about seeing any whales out of the ocean either."

Lauritzen said seals and sea lions have sometimes strayed into the fresh water. The only other time that a whale had been recorded in a river, at least on this part of the globe, was when a killer whale turned into Oregon's Willamette River in 1931. The Willamette is a tributary of the Columbia River, so the orca had to take several wrong turns. *The Los Angeles Times* quoted a man named Ed Lessard as saying the whale was sixteen feet long, and nicknamed "Ethelbert." It further quotes him as saying he killed the blasted thing. Lessard was said to have shot the beast, spiked him with a harpoon, and hauled him ashore with a net. He finally put the animal in a tank containing a preservation agent, and charged admission for a peek. He was then arrested, reportedly, and convicted of killing a fish illegally; that verdict was ultimately overturned, however, on the grounds that a whale is not a fish. A whale is a mammal.

That means the Oregon orca was more of a relation to Mr. Lessard than it was a sideshow freak.

Viewed broadly, mammals are vertebrate animals, usually warm-blooded, have large brains, sweat, and bear living young that are nourished with milk from, of course, mammary glands. The Smithsonian Institution contends that there are at least nineteen extinct and nineteen living orders of Mammalia, the latter containing more than four thousand species. Big deal, of course. There are by comparison 750,000 species of insects, but never mind. Bats are mammals, more's the pity, so are camels, kangaroos, wolves, walruses, rabbits, mountain goats, elephants, star-nosed moles, baboons, gazelles, and, if you can believe it, seventeen hundred kinds of rodents.

Whales, rats and human beings. It's a curious cosmos, especially when mixed up on common turf. The humpback whale in question is at home in the Gulf of Alaska, or cruising off the coast of Madagascar. It's discombobulating to find one in Rio Vista, doing the narrows, dodging the houseboats, performing for families eating McDLTs—for more than three weeks, yet.

Where did it come from, and why? Where was it going, and for what? No one may ever be able to say. The only thing known with absolute certainty is that it defied the otherwise rigid habits of its kind. It swam out of its saliferous, if no longer pristine, environment into the lap of the human genus—San Francisco, for crying out loud. Punk rock and Tony Bennett. Berkeley and boogie. It swam through two bays, into a maze of crowded waterways, and under six formidable bridges. One guess is that it covered three hundred to four hundred miles during the twenty-six-day odyssey, including its circlings. Along the way it's safe to say that it became the best-known cetacean since Herman Melville's Moby Dick.

It's also safe to say it shan't be soon forgotten. It was that rarest of creatures, an inspiration. It was celebrated by the big candles and small, and it stopped the clock of an otherwise unhappy earth. State and federal officials paused for his arrival; generals and admirals secured the way. At least five hundred people united to work for the visitor's welfare, and tens of thousands more bore witness with their cheers. Halley's Comet be damned. The whale in the river was the most thrilling arrival from another place in 1985. A good many lives were touched for the better.

One was that of Jack Findleton, thirty-seven at the time, fishing guide, Vietnam veteran, married with two children, Elizabeth and Carrie, boisterous, ambitious, daring, and sometimes profane. He had never seen a whale up close before October of that year. He was, nonetheless, to become the best friend the beast had in the human world. He led a waterborne rescue that science and common sense say saved the large animal's life.

"It was a Monday," Jack says. "That was the first time I heard about it. I note that because the subject came up during *Monday Night Football*. I was going to go fishing the next day, so I had driven to Rio Vista from my home in Sacramento. Fishing starts early, darlin', six A. M. I don't like to waste time driving to my boat, so I sleep on it.

"Anyway, I worked on the boat a little. Then I decided to get something to eat, watch a little football, and go to bed early. I went to Tony's Pizzeria. That's down the street from the Rio Vista Bridge. Tony has a big-screen television. The Jets were playing the Dolphins. I remember because I was born in New York. The Jets used to be my team of teams.

"Ken O'Brien had a good night. The running back, Freeman McNeil, was also hot. I asked Tony what was good on the menu. He said the meatballs were fresh. I ordered a sandwich and beer, and he asked me if I had heard about the whale in the river. The what? 'The whale in the river. Really,' he said. I said, sure, sure, Tony, there's a whale in the river.

"The Jets did well. That was a change. They were losers the year before, and the year before that. I ate my sandwich. The meatballs were okay. Then I heard someone else talking about the whale. I thought, God, a whale? I was going fishing! Freeman McNeil rushed for over a hundred yards. I went to bed. It was a nice evening. The Jets beat Miami, twenty-three to seven."

Before Jack Findleton went to sleep, he mused, *Well, at least the whale picked an interesting place to vacation.* Indeed. The Sacramento River flows through one of the most fascinating and socially significant regions of the nation. The Sacramento River Delta, specifically, is one of the man-made wonders of America. The delta used to be an inhospitable moonscape of floodplain squalor, and for a while it was an internationally renowned "waterway of gold"; now, according to the wags, it is, among other things, a place where weekend fishermen take along a quart of whiskey for snakebites, and a couple of snakes to make the precaution worthwhile.

It's not really a place for cetaceans, however, not least of all because it is, in the historical sense, the lair of the enemy. Whales may be big, but they are vulnerable. Man may be small, but he kills what he wishes. People have been destroying whales for a thousand recorded years. Americans have done it for subsistence since the dawn of the aboriginals. When the humpback entered the Sacramento River Delta, he swam past ports, such as Richmond, where thousands of his ancestors in years past had been hauled in to be decapitated, peeled, and deboned on concrete shores that still stand testament to the controversial propensity of humanity to enforce its domination.

That domination has sometimes been synonymous with subsistence. The controversy is that it has too often been compared to simpler malevolence. The senseless killing of the orca in Oregon is one example. There has been an even better and more recent illustration in Newfoundland. Canadian writer Farley Mowat chronicled the situation in the Atlantic province in a widely read book called *A Whale For The Killing*.

Mowat wrote of events that took place near his home in Burgeo, Newfoundland in January of 1967. Briefly, a seventy-foot fin whale became trapped in a tidal pool, and residents of the area looked on it as fair game. The residents were whaling people, for the most part, or at least they had connections with the industry. Mowat says they gathered in groups, good men were they all, police and military reservists at times, and shot at the helpless whale with rifles.

Mowat describes the activity as unconscionable, cold-blooded murder: "As the day wore on, more and more boats arrived and an atmosphere of fiesta began to develop. Most people were content just to watch the show from the natural rock amphitheater which cradles [the pond]. Men, women and children, many in their Sunday best, sat or stood and watched with eyes that brightened when the whale, beginning to panic, turned into shoaly water, touched bottom, reacted in terror, and then flailed her way back to deep water again while a continuous BAM-whap...BAM...whap...BAM...whap told how well the sportsmen were doing."

Mowat writes that he tried to stop the slaughter, sometimes screaming at the participants, other times begging Canadian officials for assistance. He says the provincial and dominion governments refused, for the most part, to get involved, and scientists who could have applied pressure did not.

The writer called the whale Moby Joe. He was crushed in the final chapter to find the name inappropriate. When the riflemen of Burgeo finally killed the animal, leaving it to turn over in the pond and float on its side, Mowat saw that the eighty thousand pound whale was female and, worse, pregnant.

Afterward, Mowat says his wife Clair wrote an epilogue in her journal: "How sad we are on this bright and lovely day," she wrote. Burgeo looks so beautiful, and I don't care anymore. Our whale is gone. We sat together and listened to the radio news accounts and I could not stop thinking about the savage mentality of the men who stood around the pond and emptied their rifles into that huge and harmless animal. Surely *they* are the beasts, not the whale."

Farley Mowat was contacted by phone when the humpback swam into the Sacramento River Delta. He was delighted to be told that the whale was being protected this time, in fact assisted by its hosts. He said that human beings may be learning belatedly to be human: "We've learned enough about whales to know they live in an almost perfect environment. A lot of people wish they could be like whales, roll around in the deep, and sing beautiful songs. It's a happy thought in an unhappy world."

Check. Mowat got it right. The whale drifted into the delta at what was otherwise a rotten moment on the beach. Nineteen eighty-five had been a stretch to regret. It started when a Soviet cruise missile escaped control and flew ominously over Norway and Finland, and it ended with a volcanic eruption in Colombia that buried at least ten thousand innocents.

The wars raged on, too, in El Salvador, Nicaragua, Afghanistan, Southeast Asia. The dead in the Iran-Iraq fighting reached more than a million, and the combat in Lebanon passed its eleventh year. One car bomb alone mutilated eighty men and women in Beirut. A national magazine printed photographs of children who stepped on old bombs in Southeast Asia. Communist troops in East Germany killed an American major in the continuing superpower confrontation, and police and blacks clashed in the South African argument over the right to define humanity by race rather than worth.

Eleven people were bombed to death by Philadelphia police. Perhaps twenty thousand died in cyclones in Bangladesh and earthquakes in Mexico. Officials reported that as many as one-third of America's two and a half million farmers were threatened with bankruptcy, a half dozen spies were arrested for peddling the secrets of American security, and more than two thousand passengers and crew members were killed in the worst string of commercial air disasters in history.

Then there were the terrorists. The whale swam into San Francisco Bay just after Arab thugs hijacked the luxury liner *Achille Lauro,* and a few months following the taking of a TransWorld Airlines plane. The Arabs held 153 from the plane for seventeen days and killed a nineteen-year-old American marine. They held four hundred people on the *Achille Lauro* for three days, and beat, before fatally shooting, a sixty-three-year-old tourist in a wheelchair.

Jack Findleton says he didn't think much about the whale at first. After a while, he came to love the bulky stranger. He had done a lot of killing in Vietnam. This would prove to be an opportunity to make some amends. Richard Paddock, a Los Angeles writer, quoted sociologist Neil Smelser as saying that the humpback whale was "carrying the emotional identification of our whole civilization." An exaggeration? Maybe. "This is a huge, powerful, monstrous beast floundering around helpless. It excites ambivalence in people's minds."

That ambivalence began officially on October 10. The Coast guard station at San Francisco received several similar reports that the whale, which may have left the ocean the evening before, was swimming around Angel Island, five miles due north of Fisherman's Wharf. Others who saw the animal alerted the California Marine Mammal Center (CMMC), a private group that is organized to save marine mammals in trouble. Salley Graves of the CMMC tracked the cetacean to within fifty yards of Fort Cronkhite Beach, on the north end of the Golden Gate Bridge, and she identified it as a baleen whale, that is to say toothless, a megaptera novaeangliae (humpback).

Nothing else could be said then, and even later, when physical descriptions were given, they were the product of educated guesswork. No one would examine the whale by touch during its entire sojourn in the Delta; hence no one could so much as be positive about its sex. A marine biologist named Deborah Ferrari made some early conclusions that were based on close observations, and her findings will be used for the sake of simplification throughout this recapitulation.

The biologist said the whale had probably been migrating south for the winter from waters near Alaska. Humpbacks have one of the longest migratory routes of any animal on earth. In the Pacific, they feed on summer groceries in places like the Bering Strait, and travel to Hawaii or the coast of Mexico when the weather changes. The migration is much the same for humpbacks that inhabit the Atlantic Ocean and the Antarctic Ocean, except the former vacation in the West Indies, or thereabouts, and the latter prefer Australia and New Zealand.

Debbie Ferrari said the whale in the delta was easily characterized by the hump on its back and the pectoral fins behind the corners of its mouth. The fins can grow as long as fifteen feet. They look like the wings of a Lear jet. The humpback also has the nose of a plane. It is not rounded, as is the idealistic whale of the cartoonists, but rather it is long and sleek, something like that of an alligator, and it is covered with bumps the size of truncated soccer balls.

The biologist decided the whale was male, probably young, yet fully grown. Its length was forty to forty-two feet and it weighed forty to forty-five tons, or eighty thousand to ninety thousand pounds. It was black, or nearly so, and its back was scarred, probably from scuffling with other males during mating seasons, and, let's say it now, it was nobody's patsy.

Officials at the CMMC asked Debbie Ferrari to make contact with the whale the first day. She agreed, but the whale wasn't consulted. When the biologist teamed with the Coast Guard to coax the animal back to whence it came, it refused to be crowded. It swam around Alcatraz Island, a federal penitentiary until 1963. It made passes at Treasure Island, a military encampment today. Then it "fluked." In other words, it raised its tail, it dived, and it vanished for the night.

The whale, then, had a mind of its own, and it would, at length, get a name to go with it. Jack Findleton would call it Spout for a while. The newspapers initially referred to it as E.T. (Extra Terrestrial). At one junction, country-music addicts christened the beast Delta Dawn, but nitpicking scientists preferred Wanda, as in wandering. Finally, the mass media settled on Humphrey, for obvious reasons, which precipitated the distinct bending of some noses, and the ruination of the entrepreneurs attached to them.

One merchant, for instance, had hundreds of T-shirts imprinted with the name E.T. When that handle fell from favor he was left with the unsold inventory. He implored reporters to revive the name, so he could revive his fortunes, but to no avail. He is said still to be driving around the delta, the shirts in his trunk, selling occasionally to migrant Mexican farm workers who presumably do not read English.

The fate of that peddler, by the way, was exceptional. In the main, Humphrey might well have been named Cash & Carry. The whale attracted tens of thousands of spectators, who cordially spent hundreds of thousands of dollars in the delta. One couple in Rio Vista actually insists that the sea creature came upriver specifically to save their business.

Meet Joel and Joyce Everett. They own the Little Darling's Bakery, just back from the riverfront. He is a short man with a moustache who can make a frosting rosebud with a rolled paper funnel. She is a thin blonde who wears gold earrings in the shape of a cross. They bake most of the sweet stuff at night and sell it seven days a week. They say until Humphrey came into their lives they were wearily going broke.

The reason was the California Lottery. Mr. Everett says it began operation on October 3, 1985, and quickly stole a passel of his customers. Californians spent eighty million dollars during the first week of gambling—that's the fastest start in the history of state lotteries—and the bakers in Rio Vista claim the money was siphoned away from small-trades folk:

"We can show you the receipts. We were doing fairly well before the lottery began, and we nosedived after. Bakery goods are not a necessity; they are luxury items. People tend to buy them with money left over, so here comes the lottery and all of a sudden people started buying tickets with the money left over. It was awful. Business just bombed."

Joyce Everett says the bills couldn't be paid. People were winning three-million-dollar prizes in the lottery, but the doughnuts in the Little Darling's Bakery were moldering in the case. Mrs. Everett says she worried about the rents, the lights, and, most seriously, the taxes. It's not like things could wait until the gambling novelty subsided; a cupcake has little shelf life and bismarcks do not wait for time nor tide.

Then Humphrey appeared out of nowhere in the early morning river fog, and the bakery became a concession at an assembling circus. The Everetts say it was "mystic." It was, if you'll pardon the expression, as if they had hit the lottery. Some business was only transient, expectedly, but the Everetts won back some drifters, and acquired new customers from the surrounding communities. They jubilantly proclaim they have never sold so many frosted brownies.

Sometimes the Everetts say they wish that the whale was still in the river, but they know scientifically it was out of its element. Jack Findleton says everyone in the delta got a crash course in cetacean education. Some learned more about whales than they ever wanted to, others could not get enough. John Passerello of the California Office of Emergency Services (OES) says that for the first time in his recollection, children were asking to read their parents' newspapers. Television wasn't adequate to the task. Forget the comic books. "Hey, dad, this is a veddy literate piece by George Will."

Jack Findleton tells of the day he was asked to talk about the whale with a class at the Lincoln Elementary School in Sacramento. Fourth grade, nine- and ten-year-olds—rapt attention, for a change. "They were cute as hell. I was busy at the time, but I wouldn't have passed up the opportunity. I mean, they asked me questions like, 'Mr. Findleton, did Humphrey have any brothers and sisters?'

The teacher said the kids were in awe of the animal, and they were very concerned about his well-being. She said that every day, right after the Pledge of Allegiance, the kids would remain standing and yell at the top of their voices: "Humphrey go home! Humphrey go home! Humphrey go home!"

Ah, tots. Such faith; yet thousands of grown-ups came to shout much the same thing in the delta, and millions joined in around the world. Ironic, that. People used to kill whales by the legion, merely to make shoe polish in some instances, and now, quite astonishingly, the sentiment was exactly reversed. The federal government sent a security man to protect the humpback from the first day it was sighted in the delta. The Coast Guard put men at the ready who were already overloaded with assignments, and, prophetically, people began calling up state and private agencies to volunteer boats, academic expertise, and physical labor where needed.

Debbie Ferrari continued to monitor the whale's movements at the mouth of the delta. She was accompanied by her husband, Mark. They had been summoned to the scene by the California Marine Mammal Center. Neither had a doctorate in the field, but they had a federal permit to research whales, and had extensive experience. She had become a specialist by studying humpbacks in Hawaii, several months a year for a decade. He had picked up a professional's knowledge during the same studies, beginning as a wildlife photographer. They were both thirty-five years old when Humphrey came inland, and, stretching academic formalities a little, they shall be referred to as biologists as well as researchers in these pages.

One point in passing. Debbie is the expert. Mark is public relations. She agonized over the big mammal; he got their names in print. Another biologist used to get waxed when he saw Mark Ferrari being introduced on television as an expert. "He's only an expert in promotion. He never missed a chance to beat his drum. He works for a salami company, for instance, and when the cameras came around, he always put on a cap with his company logo. I think the press missed a good chance with that. Here is a fellow who wants to save whales, but he makes his living from people who kill pigs. Pardon me, there's a wee contradiction there."

Contradiction or no, the Ferraris were tireless in the Humphrey effort, and they were instrumental in arranging the rescue effort to come. They knew after the second day that the whale had not just swum into San Francisco Bay for a bit of a rest. They decided that it was either sick, injured, or mentally unbalanced, and that it was in the delta to stay.

The biologists didn't know what exactly to do, however, particularly when the beast brushed off attempts to lure it south to the ocean. The animal appeared to be healthy. It wasn't discolored or erratic, but it wandered aimlessly, from here to there, Raccoon Strait to Richmond. Mark said it looked for a while as if it would go into Berkeley Harbor, a messy area with the depth of a swimming pool. "Thank God, it didn't." Instead, little by little, it kept edging north, toward the Sacramento River Delta.

That was alarming, and the Ferraris began to call experts to confirm what they already knew. They phoned Dr. Ken Norris, a University of California marine mammalogist with thirty years' experience; John Twiss, director of the Marine Mammal Commission of the United States; Dr. Lou Herman, professor of Marine Mammal Behavior at the University of Hawaii; and Dr. Bill Watkins of the Woods Hole Oceanographic Institution.

The experts were as one in their thinking. If Humphrey proceeded into the delta, he would run out of saltwater. If he ran out long enough, he would probably perish.

The salt matter is curious. It's also confusing. On the one hand, cetaceans must have salt water; on the other hand, being mammals, they need fresh water as well. So why was Humphrey in danger? Dr. Watkins of Woods Hole explains:

"First, the freshwater requirement. Like humans, whales require pure moisture to sustain tissue and cell life, but unlike Humphrey, they do not normally go cavorting in the good stuff. Watkins says whales live off their metabolic water, the liquid that is manufactured in all animals from the chemical breakdown of food sugars and other carbohydrates.

"Now the need for the saline solution. A constant supply is imperative. One reason is that it's a function of a process known as osmotic regulation. That is what prevents whales from becoming waterlogged. Salt water creates pressure that regulates the amount of moisture that seeps through the cetacean skin—it's waterproofing, if you will—and fresh water will allow that seepage to intensify into leaks."

Thus Humphrey was undoubtedly heading for woe. The salt content of the ocean averages from twenty-nine to thirty-five parts per thousand. The salt content of the Sacramento River Delta ranges from nine parts to zero. Humphrey's skin started to get sodden the first two days he was in San Francisco Bay. Dr. Watkins says the skin of dolphins kept in fresh water deteriorates seriously within a week to ten days. That deterioration is reasonably thought to be the beginning of the end.

Dr. Watkins says when skin tissue bloats, it drowns. When

that occurs, the skin begans to sluff, or break apart. That condition creates subsequent internal reactions that affect organs. No one knows how long it takes for expiration. No one knows much about whales, except how to hunt them. It was widely assumed, however, that Humphrey the Wayward Whale was absolutely on a death cruise in the Sacramento River Delta.

chapter two

WHEN ISHMAEL WAS TO GET ON THE RECORD IN MELville's *Moby Dick,* he called for the appropriate tools. "Give me a condor's quill!" he shouted. "Give me Vesuvius' crater for an inkstand," and no wonder. One might use a Parker to describe ordinary animals, he was saying, but it should take something more to put the great whales to paper. They are the most superlative beasts the world has ever known. They defy the fleeting word. They are the largest and heaviest animals on earth, for one thing. They are likewise among the most traveled and intelligent. Most curiously, they are, in at least one respect, closely related to another amazing creature, man, and are quite like him in other ways too.

That's not to say, as many do, that cetaceans are overfed "humans of the seas." The similarities between the types fall short of this happy thought; yet people and whales emerged from the same primordial soup, and they remain akin to the same fundamental mammal stock. Of course, the two animals took different evolutionary routes: man stayed on his feet to become the governing life on land; the cetaceans returned to the waters from where they originated to dominate existence in the oceans.

The term cetacean is from a Greek word "ketos" and a Latin word "cetus," both meaning whale. It is used to classify the creatures who probably developed from carnivores sixty to sixty-five million years ago. Scientists are not certain what the whales looked like while they still had legs, but a good wager is that they were more like hippopotami than felines. The whales probably went back to the seas very soon after their initial development, for reasons of which no one has the slightest clue, and they have spent the intervening millennium adapting a waterborne (read it: fishy) superstructure.

They still share some characteristics with the primates of the past and present. They have smooth skin rather than scales. They can grow hair and are warm-blooded. The whale's flipper is the functional remains of a forepaw. Its nostrils have migrated to the top of its head to become blowholes. It has eyes, ears, and communication habits more closely resembling those of man than those of pickerel. The ear has become entirely internal, for reasons of aerodynamics. The eye is movable and lidded, and some species have stereoscopic capabilities, meaning they can view a single subject in three dimension.

Then there's the sex. It is also much the same with whales as with people. A large male whale may have a three-foot penis, and the ladies of the deep are deep and how, but otherwise, there are striking similarities. Writer Nicolas Rosa described them in a 1984 article in *Oceans* magazine:

There they float, like balloons in the water. How do they get a grip on the problem? Humpback whales, with their long, winglike flippers, can "stand" like humans and clasp each other. In the gray whales, a courting trio is involved... It is hard to see what is going on, but some witnesses say a second (assistant? apprentice?) male places his body across the nose of the female, halting her progress in the water.

I have watched gray whales mating in the opaque green waters off central California in which the (presumed) female swims prone at the surface and the (supposed) bull is upside down underneath, with his tail flukes alongside her tailstock. Whale-watching cruises are sometimes X-rated; we have seen bull grays, in triumph, frustration, exultation or confusion, rolling at the surface...exposed to the breeze. We have counted at one time up to eight romping gray whales.

Now, among the southern right whales, a female in an amorous mood is approached by her chosen male, who dives beneath her and rolls over, belly up. As his body nears hers, his erect penis comes out of the genital slit like some devilish Wehrmacht field rocket launcher and, with uncanny aim, he glides up into full belly-to-belly contact with his bride. The two whales clasp each other with their stuffy flippers and their tails begin to beat in unison. Their movement is graceful. I understand that couplings last about eight seconds. Then the male uncouples, comes up for air, and dives again to repeat the action.

Whew. Author Rosa says the shenanigans may go on for a couple of hours. Calves may be born in ten to sixteen months. The young are deposited live in the water and pushed to the surface for the breath of life. The babies are usually very large at birth, to give them every chance in the environment. Humpback calves weigh at least a ton. A dolphin's weight may increase by a factor of seven in the first year. The sperm whale, it's said, can grow from a barely visible egg to twenty-nine tons in less than two years; the mathematicians say that is an increase of thirty billion times.

Cetaceans are classified in two primary groups today. The Odontoceti, or toothed whales, include sixty-five or more species of dolphins, porpoises, and whales with molars. The Mysticeti, or baleen whales, include ten species of the more classic animals, such as humpbacks. *The Guinness Book of World Records* says that the largest cetacean ever accurately measured was a female sperm whale that stretched more than 110 feet and weighed, exclusive of blood, a staggering 366,000 pounds.

It took Humphrey three days to swim into what would become a most serious predicament. The problem in San Francisco Bay was that he might be injured by the boating traffic. The problem in San Pablo Bay was that he was traveling away from adequate salt. When he reached the Sacramento River Delta itself, the risks began to multiply exponentially: the waters were not as deep, the banks began to line with unpredictable spectators, and the river branched into a confounding maze of hostile sloughs, trickles, and closures.

As a consequence, the Coast Guard called for additional assistance. By October 14, a government helicopter had been dispatched to observe the creature's movements from the air. The Contra Costa Sheriff's Office put a boat in the water, and the California Fish and Game Department arrived to observe and assist in a vessel of its own. The Coast Guard said the whale was "disoriented." A sheriff's officer thought it was "very sick." People on the shorelines had a laundry list of opinions. The biologists, however, made the most telling assessment; Mark Ferrari said they were beginning to learn how little they really knew.

There was one other possibility regarding the whale's behavior, and a distinct one, given the history of the order. Whales have been known to strand themselves on beaches, or in shallows, for as long as men and women have been observing them. They have cast themselves on shores individually, or in large numbers, sometimes with an apparent purpose, and the peculiarity has led to a great deal of popular speculation, most of it guesstimation, and part of it rhapsody.

Some people believe cetaceans may hear a genetic siren calling them or have some other kind of inherited urge to return to the land. The theory has some documented support. Whales will occasionally follow one another to the sand or the rocks, even though they are intelligent enough to see and perhaps even understand what they are doing. Then, when they are fortunate enough to be set adrift by tides, or led back to deep water by people, they may refuse to swim to freedom.

Needless to say, no one comprehends the matter, but the implications are so enormous that scientists tend to look for simpler explanations. Mammalogists say that most landlocked whales probably miscalculate the tides or the depth of the water, while avoiding a predator, say, or while following food in a current. Alternatively, the thinking is that whales may beach themselves because of physical malfunctions; their navigation systems break down so that they can't find their way around.

That's science. Always trying to reduce the complex to the impossible. Can a whole herd (pod) of whales have navigation troubles at once? Can thirty or forty beasts get so interested in dinner that they accidentally slide onto the shore all at once? Man has gone back to the sea, for a look; the possibility that marine mammals make similar probes is not beyond the fanciful. Humphrey may have, therefore, come upriver to see what was what or, more grotesquely, to impale himself suicidally upon the ancient graveyard.

Jack Findleton was fishing while dismay about the whale was building. He still had scant interest in the developing theatrics.

The weather was warm, the water was cooperating, and he had set out in his fishing boat, Sportfish I, a twenty-four-foot Bayliner with single screw drive, in search of striped bass.

I had invited Bob King to join me. He used to be a police captain and we had fished together before. I remember we turned south out of Rio Vista and anchored at the mouth of Three Mile Slough. A slough is a tributary. Tributaries vary in size and scope. Back east they call them creeks.

Well, we didn't have any luck there. When we tried a couple of other areas, we still didn't have any luck—not a bite, not a nibble. Some people had said the whale might chase the fish away. I thought about that. I make my living on the water. I mean, hey, we didn't get a single fish.

So we were sitting there. It was like the bait wasn't even trying. Then, lo and behold, there was the whale. It was going down the river, followed by a Coast Guard launch and some other boats. It seemed to be having a nice time. I would say it was frolicking, rolling in and out of the water.

I had seen whales before on television, but this was the first time in the flesh. I couldn't see very much of him. He never came out of the water, but seeing the hump on his back was enough. I was excited. The biggest animal I'd ever seen was a few thousand pounds. This sucker was like a dream.

I said, "There it is, Bob."

He said, "Christ," or words to that effect.

We looked until it was gone. Then we went home, empty-handed, goddamn it, but by then I wasn't thinking about the fish anymore. Instead, I was thinking about the whale. The delta is a big place, and it's like a spider web. I began to realize that Humphrey may be caught in the strands.

The analogy is appropriate. The Sacramento River Delta is a big, as well as a tangled, formation. It is something of a remarkably risky monument as well. Humphrey's ancestors would have seen it as a wilderness swamp until a century ago. It was an endless level of muck, while the native Indians still kept the watch. The delta began as the confluence of the Sacramento and San Joaquin rivers. That much has not changed, but the wild and sodden moors have been salvaged for development, the tules and bulrushes of antiquity have yielded the way to commercial agriculture, and the remarkable hand of Everyman has reclaimed 750,000 of the most important and perhaps most tenuous acres in America.

The reclamation started in the second half of the 1800s, between the time gold was discovered in the rivers of the region (1848) and the time the transcontinental rail line was built from the East Coast to San Francisco (1869). The gold miners found that there wasn't enough precious metal to go around, and the Chinese who worked on the railroad were left to search for new horizons when the construction was completed. The delta was known as "the New Netherlands" then; it had the look of the Zuider Zee in Holland. When the unemployed armies looked around at the pickings, the delta marsh seemed the most promising place to settle. The Chinese and the miners combined muscle and enterprise, respectively, and both were utilized to transform the delta.

The job was not easy. An early settler wrote in his diary that he could suffer neither the remaining Indians nor the mosquitoes. Then there was the floodplain itself. The rivers meandered at will, most of all when swollen by rains or melting snow, and they were backed all the way to Sacramento by the tides from the Pacific Ocean. The streambeds were also complicated by debris. Silt was a given, and almost two billion yards of gold-mine tailings were dumped in the delta in the latter part of the century. Even so, the peat soil was some of the richest in the nation, but the land couldn't be used without separating it from the water.

At first, the work was done by hand. The Chinese coolies built three-foot levees around selected pieces of property. Then the machinery was added. The Chinese are supposed to have reclaimed 107,000 acres with wheelbarrows by 1880, but when the assignments were mechanized, the project became fully historic. Construction on the Panama Canal began in 1904; it was the only place on earth where more people and equipment were assembled on a single digging enterprise.

Today the reclaimed delta is a network of islands formed by high, wide, and commercially handsome levees. The waters are controlled, where possible, by channels and dams. The area forms the shape of a triangle, like the Greek letter delta. It runs roughly from Sacramento on the north, to Stockton on the south, to San Francisco on the west. There are a score of towns and settlements throughout the delta, but most of the island space is given over to farms and ranches. Large corporations and small families grow potatoes, tomatoes, sugar beets, asparagus, beans, melons, squash, onions, celery, Bartlett pears, et cetera, and scattered herds of cattle and sheep graze under the protection of the dykes.

Repeat. *Under* the protection of the dykes. The islands in the delta are still in large part composed of peat, and so they sink, burn off, and partly blow away in cycles. The measured belief is that the peat islands are subsiding at a rate of one inch every four years. The result is that most of them are now lower than the surrounding streams. Boats on the Sacramento River float higher than the corn that grows just across the levees, and Humphrey the Whale swam as high as some roofs. Residents say the whole arrangement is perfectly safe unless the endlessly anticipated California earthquake strikes; in that case, cetaceans who might decide to travel here in the future would most likely have the delta, once more in its original design, to themselves.

By now, the presence of the cetacean was common knowledge in the delta. The news media recognized the story on the third and fourth days, and word of the adventure was sent to the front porches and the living rooms of the world. Housewives kept their children home from school to have whale-watching picnics on the banks of the Sacramento. Clerks and farmers spent their lunchtimes probing the water with cameras and binoculars. There were even witnesses at night, after a fashion, when fishermen and business people collected for reflection and discussion at river-town pubs.

Many of the discussions centered on the question of what to do about the damned thing. Lines were being drawn to bracket a pair of opposite views. The first was that the animal should be left alone to sink or swim, in keeping with the laws of nature, and the second was that the beast should be inspected, protected, and, if possible, given help to get back home. Very few people talked of destroying the creature, a la Moby Joe in the Newfoundland tidal pond. Rio Vista fisherman Dick Whitehead says, however, that there were some grunts made about "sharpening knives for the blubber." Joel Everett of the Little Darling's Bakery adds that he saw young people tormenting Humphrey in miniature hydroplanes. Otherwise, the overwhelming consensus was affable and benevolent.

There's irony in that. The Sacramento River Delta is a recreational as well as an agricultural preserve. The residents own more firearms than do the governments of many nations. They hunt bear in the Sierra Mountains, deer in the coastal hills, and ducks in "The New Netherlands." "Real men" in the region wear beards or, at least, moustaches. They also load their own shells, and believe that killing is a serious sport. The local joke is about two guys in a boat, in the hot sun, hour after hour. One of them says, "Herb, son of a bitch, that's the second time you've moved your feet today. Are you out here to fish or to dance?"

The best-known watering hole in Rio Vista is Foster's Bighorn. Kay Woodson, an assistant to the area's United States Representative, calls it "the bar of death." It was built by the late William Foster, who was obsessed with safari hunting. He killed in Africa. He killed in Alaska. He killed in South America. What's more, he stuffed the heads of his prey and mounted them throughout his restaurant.

There are three hundred stuffed heads, birds, and fish in Foster's Bighorn. They peer down with glass eyes at the patrons. There is an elephant that measures thirteen feet from the neck to the outstretched trunk and a moose with an antler spread of seventy-six inches. Regular customers say the display is enough to drive one to drink. There is a cheetah, a lion, a wildebeest, a rhinoceros, a leopard, ad infinitum and absurdum.

Bwana Foster died in 1963, leaving all heads but his own on the wall. Those who remember him say he could detail every trifle of every shot he ever fired. He was a local celebrity in his time, which has mercifully passed. The restaurant now provides a businessman's lunch for under five dollars. Jack Findleton said it was for sale in 1985. Humphrey at least chose a good time to come up the river; thirty years ago he would have made the biggest trophy of all over the tables at the bar of death.

But let's not make too much of the obscene. Rio Vista is by and large a friendly and progressive place. The community was founded in 1858 at a site four miles upriver from the present location; it was relocated, actually swept downwater, during an 1862 flood. Rio Vista was then called the capital of the New

Netherlands. It is now the second city in Solano County, and in 1985 it was the unofficial home away from home of Humphrey the whale.

Frankly, Humphrey hung around several river towns during his sojourn in the delta, such as Antioch, Benica, Martinez, Vallejo. Nobody took to him as did the people of Rio Vista. "We adopted him," says Sally Downs, the proprietor of the town's principal fishing and sundry shops. "He was *our* whale," adds Chamber of Commerce manager Diana Del-Zampo. Michael Swigart, a forty-year-old engineering technician, goes one step more: "Humphrey was a visitor from far away. He was looking for intelligent life and so he came to Rio Vista."

The intelligent life numbers about three thousand, according to the travel brochures, and thirty-one thousand to thiry-three thousand sayeth the sticklers. The town is sixty-five miles northeast of San Francisco, forty miles southwest of Sacramento. There is one bridge, one newspaper, 250 agriculture services, 150 manufacturing concerns, and, as the Humphrey press corps found to their horror, only three public telephones. There are also three schools, 350 retail stores, and an average temperature of sixty-one degrees.

Sounds small. Backwater, even. It is and it isn't. Milton Wallace, the mayor who is never called Milton, says the biggest event in Rio Vista is the annual striped bass derby, and that's just fine with him. He is a retired shipmaster; he says he was at sea for fourteen years, and he underscores fourteen. "I don't count the years I was employed; I only count the years I was on the water." He is a gnarled and unguarded fellow, given to the constant realignment of his floppy-billed cap, and he wears work pants and white socks to the municipal building. "We get four to five thousand at the bass derby, and they don't just fish. There are raffle wheels and Portuguese beans. Everybody has a really good time."

Sally Downs does, for example. She sponsors a bass derby queen contest. She sells bait and supplies to the boats. She also has a popular open house at her fine home, and throws sophisticated parties for interesting guests. She represents another face of tiny, outback Rio Vista. She used to be an advertising executive in Los Angeles; now she peddles worms and plastic poppers.

She says she followed her husband to Rio Vista. "I have to

say I did not want to get into the bait business." Her husband died, however, and she inherited the shops. Now she's made peace with two worlds. She is a short, Rubenesque woman, who wears designer spectacles on a chain around her neck. She is a popular, gregarious hostess who is comfortable in tennis shoes, on the one foot, but keeps her fingernails manicured.

Downs has her nails done at Mane Street Hair in Rio Vista. The town is not too out of the way to be fashionable. Fingernails are the rage in California. Cuticle maintenance is chi chi. Charlene Paine, who owns Mane Street Hair, says most of the women who come in for permanents also have their nails shaped and flattered. It's not just a quick dip in the Palmolive, either. It is like major reconstruction.

The fad is said to have started some years ago. It may have been introduced by Vietnamese refugees after the events in Southeast Asia. There are hundreds of Vietnamese manicurists in California now, most of them raised to believe that fine nails are feminine, sexy too, so they insist, though the jury is still out. At any rate, Mane Street Hair charges forty dollars to do nails the first time, and twenty dollars for repairs.

Charlene Paine says some women have work done on their own equipment, but the normal procedure is to, um, use falsies. Plastic nails are stronger, after all, and uniform. The nails are pasted on, shaped if desired, and painted every color from amber to blueberry. The popular length is one inch, though some prefer even longer claws. When the regular nails grow, of course, the fakes are pushed along, and epoxy fillers are used to fill in the cuticle gaps.

Is everyone still reading? This gets better. Beautician Paine says her customers may also opt to wear fingernail jewelry. That's what the punk rockers started, and the trend has gone at least as far as Rio Vista. Some manicurists can insèt gold and silver designs in the nails; others apply tack-on objects, such as small charms and decals. Initials are nice, so are plain diamonds. There are pornographic drawings for the bold, and horoscope logos for the Republicans. Whatever happened to Avon? Paine says women today can drop as much as one thousand dollars on a trip to the beauty shop.

No one on the boats watching Humphrey wore fingernail jewelry. Debbie Ferrari, the biologist, tends to chew rather than pamper her talons. Humphrey was still wandering around the lower part of the Sacramento River. Coaxing had not worked. Herding had not worked, so on October 14, Ferrari brought in something to scare the animal back toward the ocean: taped sounds of migrating killer whales.

The tapes were supplied by a pair of graduate students from the University of California at Santa Cruz. Michael Poole specializes in gray whales, and David Baines is trained in acoustics. Baines had recorded the orca sounds earlier. Both men told of experiments where orca sounds had caused dolphins and gray whales to "get worried and turn from their courses." Orcas can be dangerous. They make sounds like angry lions roaring in the jungle.

The sounds were fed to underwater equipment, which were in turn broadcast toward Humphrey. The equipment was not the best, and no one knew if the whale heard the tapes or not, or whether he was affected or not. The upshot was that the sounds did not work as hoped, or at all. Humphrey continued to meander in the river, following his own orchestra.

Maybe the whale was deaf. Things were getting curiouser and curiouser. "What do you know about this business?" the King of Hearts asked Alice. "Nothing whatsoever," she replied. "That's very important," he concluded.

No description of a small town is complete without a rural joke. A Rio Vista farmer went to a hardware store to order seventy-eight axe handles at two dollars apiece. He said he was going to sell them to his neighbor for one dollar each. But, sir, the clerk said, it's ridiculous to lose a dollar on every sale. "Sure is," the man agreed, "but it beats farming."

Jack Findleton got a call from Bob King. He said a photographer from San Francisco wanted to take a picture of Humphrey, and was looking for a boat to charter. Jack said he was available. He could use the money, and he wouldn't have to spring for the usual bait. That was how he got involved, by chance, obliquely, in saving the whale.

Tuesday, October 15. It was becoming clear that the whale needed saving, but arguments regarding the question would continue to parent hesitation. The monitors were increasing in number; scientists across the nation were being consulted, and the California Marine Mammal Center was preparing for an emergency. Still, no one had any authority to do anything other than observe and contemplate, even if they had known what to do besides observe and contemplate.

The Ferraris went hunting for Humphrey by helicopter. The participating Coast Guard craft stemmed out of Rio Vista on the same mission. Media crews and recreational skippers were also on the water, searching for the whale that had turned the wrong way, the Mysticeti that couldn't navigate straight, the ocean inhabitant that was not a fish, and the beast whom one Walter Dwyer of Waterford believed could be rescued in a "huge plastic sack" towed to the Pacific by a tug.

Humphrey was found in the morning.

Everyone's heart sank.

He was stranded off land known as Decker Island.

Peigin Barrett explains what that meant. She is the executive director of CMMC, and she has been involved with numerous sea mammal strandings. First, she says, the whale probably beached because the tide was low and it was not familiar with the area. Second, the reason didn't matter. It was on killing ground.

Barrett says she had just completed a study course in miracles before the Humphrey saga. Now that seemed terribly apropos. She says whales out of water do not die of exposure; they die by suffocation. Humphrey needed water for buoyancy. On the beach, he was entombed by his unsupported weight — eighty thousand pounds or more, the bulk of a small house. Barrett says the weight would eventually settle, break his ribs, crush his lungs, and inhibit breathing.

The biologists were miserable. There was little if anything that could be done. Someone thought about using at least one part of Walter Dwyer's plan, pulling the beast free with a tugboat, but that might hasten collapse of the whale's weight. The only other consideration was to make the whale as comfortable as possible. It hadn't been many months before that villagers in New Zealand had rescued a pod of 360 pilot whales that had become stranded on an island; they did it by keeping the animals wet, to prevent sunburn, and guiding them free when the tide cooperated.

The biologists made preparations. Barrett had stocked

sheets to cover the whale, and zinc oxide ointment to prevent sunburn. Mark Ferrari called for a tugboat from Rio Vista. Hope was faint, however, and spectators stood about, kicking dirt. Cynthia Barker, a waitress from Rio Vista, revealed that she had seen the whale acting strangely the night before, "hitting poles and other stuff." Ruth McMonagee from Pittsburg added, "I wish he would do some moving." Vivian Prieb of Isleton was also on hand, shaking her head. "Poor guy," she said, "he just wants to go back home."

chapter three

SOMEONE LACKING CHARITY ONCE SAID THAT THE GREATEST service we can do the common man is to abolish him. That would have been the end of John Young Findleton. The Sacramento fisherman is the quintessential ordinary fellow. He has a good side, a bad side, and a side that is still being considered. He works for wages, struggles with a mortgage, and he is as functional as a ball-peen hammer. He can be explosive, often profane, and cries like an innocent child. Don't look for pious nobility here. If he's a hero, it's like the responsible cop on the block. Jack led the physical effort to rescue Humphrey the Whale. If he hadn't, it would have had to have been done by another in the proletariat, a common man capable of uncommon things, just like him.

"I didn't know my backside from a hat rack," he says regarding his role. "I was also too dumb to know when to quit."

Persistence. Jack was raised to the cloth. He grew up in Port Washington, N.Y., on Long Island, near the water, the mother of life and therefore perseverance. He was born in 1948. The Baby Boom was in swing. The Yankees and the Giants were champions of the world. The war was two years over. Harry Truman was president. The Kinsey *Report on Sexuality in the Human Male* was published, and the earliest thing Jack remembers is his father on the job: "My dad was a part-time electrical contractor. He also worked for the power utility. I helped him as an assistant sometimes. We installed air conditioners and that kind of thing. The man busted his butt for us. There was my mom, myself, and one sister, Susan. I mean, day in, day out, year after year, he busted his butt."

The Findleton's lineage is Scotch. Jack's father taught him that if he didn't work hard, he wouldn't get anything, and even if he did work hard, he might not get much. Still, there was time for a cup or two and, of course, the water. Jack's grandfather bought him his first fishing rod and Jack constructed his first boat himself, during puberty. "I was home in Manhasset Bay. That's the bottom of Long Island Sound. We used to hunt for cherrystone clams. There's a trick to it. You stamp on the ground and wait for the clam to piss [spout through the sand]. Then you dig like mad. Clams are delicacies. I didn't eat them, though. I combined business with pleasure, and sold them to the fish bars set up on the water."

Jack passes over his years at school. He was a middling student, and played lacrosse and ice hockey in high school. But work? He can recount details to the one-hundredth power. Once, for instance, he was employed as a bill collector, and he devised a ploy he might yet have patented. This was before the age of consumer protection. Debt collection resembled guerrilla warfare. People who owed twenty-five dollars to the pharmacy got muffled calls in the middle of the night. Women and children took assumed names for safety. Everything but car bombing was practiced. Jack Findleton, ah ha, took a different approach. To wit, he killed with kindness:

There was this one guy who wouldn't pay a bill of three or four hundred dollars—something like that, and he was very snotty about it. He changed his phone, didn't give out his address, and vowed he wouldn't be taken alive. You know the kind. Anyway, I didn't get mad. I did my homework, and calmly devised a plan of operation. The first thing I found out was that he was a used-car salesman. Now I couldn't just go down there. He could have me removed from the lot by police. I called him up and said, "Look, I have a friend who bought a car from you last month; he said it was a great deal, and I was looking for an automobile myself."

That established a relationship. I was now a potential client, and we talked on and on. I flattered him some more. I said he must have an interesting job. Pretty soon the conversation turned personal. I asked him if he lived on Long Island. He said he did, in Hempstead. I said, "Isn't that a coincidence; I have an aunt who lives in Hempstead. Is his house anywhere near Rose Street?" He said no, it was Elm Street, or something. "God," I said, "I know Elm Street; what block?" When he told me, I showed up the next day, waving the bills, very politely. He knew he had been had. He got the sting. He paid the debt very sheepishly.

Jack tells the story at a high decibel, and with considerable animation. He is a man of average height, made taller by an imposing personality. Some of the people who worked with him to save the whale called him "Jack the Mouth." He admits he commanded the effort by periodically throwing his weight around. He also provided a shoulder to lean on. He drives a pickup truck, wears a thick moustache on a round face, and has to watch his weight. "I used to weigh 317 pounds at one point. I was like the man on the carnival stage, so I decided to get rid of some of it. After I lost sixty pounds, somebody pinched my backside on a dance floor. I said, hey, if they do that after sixty pounds, what will happen after one hundred? I weighed about 225 when I first saw the whale in the river, and lost fifteen pounds more chasing it around."

Speaking of hulk, the great whale was stranded on Decker Island for at least two hours. It was still partially submerged in water, over the head and the tail, but the prognosis was grim. The whale did not shift for long periods, and the exposed skin showed early signs of decay. Some people who saw the beast called police departments to demand that something be done; eventually, officials decided that the only reasonable thing to do was to wait for high water and hope the animal could wiggle loose.

That's what eventually happened. The tide rose. Humphrey thrashed about, using its enormous pectoral fins for leverage. It slid back into sufficient water in the afternoon, to the applause of those at the death watch. Once more the Mysticeti, whose Latin classification means "the big winged creature from New England," had defied the odds and survived—by itself. People had been well-intentioned but incidental, up to this point. Humphrey may have been mixed up, but he was still trucking, and he was not evidently suicidal.

When the whale cleared the shallows, he was followed triumphantly by the string of monitoring and observation vessels, official and otherwise—the biologists, the Coast Guard, the police, and sailboats, houseboats, outboard motorboats, skiffs, and dinghies. Sally Downs in Rio Vista said it was beginning to look "like the invasion of Normandy."

Jack also recognized the military similarities—from personal experience. He graduated from high school in 1966, just as the war in Southeast Asia was expanding, but before the public outrage had taken root. He enlisted in the Army. He can't say why, exactly, except he wasn't bound for college and he didn't have a career outline. Besides, he is a common man, patriot. Thank heavens for eighteen-year-old boys who want to do right by their country. He was sent to Fort Jackson, South Carolina for basic training, and he went on to airborne school (the paratroops). "I wanted to be as good as I could. Jumping from planes shapes character. They assigned me to the 101st Airborne Division, a unit that was sending people to Vietnam on every plane. I knew I was next when they issued my camouflage gear, and then strung concertina wire around the compound so that we couldn't get out and run away."

Some escaped anyway. Others pleaded instantly acquired homosexuality for relief. Jack kept the faith, though. He was scared. He didn't even know precisely where Indochina was, but he says he obeyed what he calls a code of silence: "If you worried about being blown to hell, you didn't confess it. Gallows humor was all right. Holding hands was not." Jack's outfit was transported to Guam on a C-141, a swept-wing apparition that took people to the war in fresh fatigues and brought them back in blood-filled rubber bags. The troops were issued live ammunition in Guam. Jack was sent from there to Saigon, and onward eventually to an outpost secured by the 101st near the demilitarized zone.

The Screaming Eagles. They had been the stuff of legend in World War II and Korea. They were every bit as fabled, though not, as it turned out, so useful, in South Vietnam:

"We were way in the bush. I forgot what clean sheets were. I forgot what sheets were. Our job was to search and destroy. The idea was to kill everyone else so we could stay alive ourselves. We were camped in a graveyard one night. We knew the North Vietnamese were superstitious, and we thought they would avoid the place. The officers told us to spread out, but be careful. Nobody was to disturb a stone or dig over a grave. One man said to hell with that. He rummaged around and found some buried skulls. Then he tied them through the eyeholes with a string. I asked him what he was doing, and he said if the gooks were afraid to come to the graveyard, maybe they would feel the same if the graveyard came to them. Later, when we got in a firefight, he threw the skulls at the jerks rather than grenades."

Anything went. There was a Vietnam mercenary who was given a United States bounty for each severed hand he brought in, no questions asked about proof of origin. Lieutenant William Calley would order his men to kill more than a hundred civilians in a single day, without a shot fired in return. One colonel in command would refuse to allow his helicopter to land under fire to fetch a wounded soldier, but he received a Silver Star anyway when his pilot disobeyed the order. Jack never questioned all the killing. He thought, "This is bullshit," but not in the sense of being morally right or wrong. He endured the death, and the despair, and the degeneration without a political complaint.

"Remember, I was in the deep bush. I did not hear much about the protests at home. I was surviving. It's not healthy to think you are being screwed. I figured I was fighting for my country. I was on the front lines against Communism. I still believed in the government, damn it. I thought we were winning the war."

Jack remained in combat for twelve months. He was awarded a Bronze Star for gallantry. He had gone to Vietnam with 144 people; twenty-seven of them came home alive. He left the war with a walking stick carved in the shape of an upright finger. His fiance had returned his ring by mail. He was twenty years old when he got back to Port Washington, and no one asked him where he had been. He told his mother not to startle him while he was sleeping. He went downtown and saw a candlelight parade for peace. He developed a rash on his chest, which he would eventually attribute to Agent Orange herbicide. He began to wonder why all his friends had been killed.

"I suppose that I expected everybody to run up to me and say, 'By God it's good to see you, Jack; let me buy you a drink.' That didn't happen. What happened was that I ran up to them and said, 'Let me buy the drinks, *I'm* glad to see you.' "

Jack tried college, briefly. Then he says he got married to

the first woman who showed him some appreciation and they had two children. He got a job as a bouncer in a topless bar, and then in the bill-collecting industry. All the while, he was emotionally uneasy. He had put his life on the line, while others had refused the legal obligation; yet he paid a consequence and they did not. He felt left out. He couldn't communicate with his own generation. He had been cheated. By whom? "The government," he says. "They (it) sent me to do the dirty work. They kept the war going long after it was a hopeless cause. The big men argue and the little men die. How many politicians were killed? I remember when Watergate happened. I had served that same White House for one bloody year. I bought some paint and put a big sign in my window at home. It said, "Impeach Nixon."

Humphrey was now fifty-five miles from the sea. When he left the boneyard at Decker Island, he headed north, disappeared, and emerged again near what would become another landmark on his journey: the Rio Vista Bridge. He had already encountered three spans on the trip: The Golden Gate, and two more at Carquinas Strait between San Pablo Bay and the Sacramento River. Those structures rose high off the water. The bridge at Rio Vista, on the other hand, is only twenty feet above the waves. It looks like a dam from a distance, and it rattles much of the time with noisy vehicular traffic.

Everyone thought Humphrey would stop there.

He didn't.

He swam under the bridge, and hence into a greater jam. He suddenly had a clear shot north, all the way to Sacramento. He could also have gone into a wickerwork of sloughs on the east and west flanks. The only certainty was that he did not appear to be in a hurry to go back south. He stayed around the upriver side of the Rio Vista bridge for a time, but refused to get very close. Maybe he realized that the low-slung structure was imposing; it was a fine time to come to his senses.

Jack Findleton moved to California with an occupational promotion. He had worked his way into some prominence in bill-collecting circles and was sent west to open a new agency. He says he couldn't even spell Sacramento, but there were compensations. One was the water. He rented a house early on, from which he had to motor over the American River to get to his office. He saw people fishing on the banks—it reminded him of the pastime he had left behind on Long Island—and he stopped to get a better look as well as to inquire about the local predilections.

"I asked people what they were fishing for. They said striped bass. Bingo, I knew I had found a new home. I fished striped bass most of my life in New York. I thought it was strictly an eastern fish. Turns out the fish were brought out here last century, and were dumped into the rivers. Now they are all over the place. What a fish. They'll pull you out of the boat. I've seen them forty-five to fifty pounds or more."

Jack didn't like bill collecting anyway. He knows what it's like to get a little behind himself; therefore, he decided to change his life completely. In sequence, he divorced his wife from Port Washington, he lost that weight mentioned before, he married his present wife, he put away the stiff collar of what is euphemistically known as "debt recovery," and he became a self-employed fishing guide. What everyday fellow hasn't dreamed of doing the same thing? Think of it: "What are you doing at home, Jack? You are supposed to be out fishing."

Jack takes up to four people a day on angling expeditions. Seventy-five dollars a pop, and liberal use of the head. He gets doctors, lawyers, laborers—and some wise guys.

"Fishing?"

"Yup."

"How many you caught?"

Pause.

"I said, how many you caught?"

"Well, if I get the one I'm working on now, before you scare him away, and if I get two others, I'll have three."

Jack is president of the Sacramento chapter of the California Striped Bass Association. He flies the organizational flag from the bow of his boat, so his bias is advertised. He also likes three other anadromous fish that run in the Sacramento River Delta: steelhead, salmon, and sturgeon. Steelhead are also known as ocean trout, because they live in salt water and spawn in fresh, and sturgeon are among the most primitive, ugly, and, all things considered, interesting game fish in the world.

Sturgeon have been roaming the earth's waters for millions of years. One species, the beluga, has been known to grow to twenty-eight feet in length and weigh twenty-eight hundred pounds. The genus in the Sacramento Delta has been measured at nine feet and 350 pounds. Either way, they are splendidly inelegant. They have beady eyes, flat heads, and they are lined with barbed, platelike eruptions. At best, they look like an elongated pizza. They taste like it too. Pepperoni. Next question.

Jack had been fishing for sturgeon and striped bass for just over a year when the whale photographer from San Francisco hired his boat. The next day his service was in even greater demand. The biologists and other technicians needed someone who knew the waters, so they asked Jack to take them out. He didn't hesitate to say yes. That put the Vietnam veteran and everyday bloke square in the center of the bizarre and thickening drama.

The bafflement of the moment was the Rio Vista Bridge. The whale swam under it with ease going north; yet he avoided the idea of going south. He made some passes, but aborted each time. At one point, the Coast Guard reported that the animal was "slapping" the water near the overpass, perhaps a display of tantalization. Peigin Barrett of CMMC had to know why, exactly. The bridge was like a wall in the water now. Humphrey was in effect being fenced off from the ocean. Barrett wondered about the noise on the bridge, and she called for consultants to take a look.

The consultants were Drs. Bernard Krause and Diana Reiss. He is a bioacoustical specialist from San Francisco who normally does sound work with motion pictures, *Apocalypse Now*, to name one; she is an instructor in and researcher of the science of animal and human communications. Krause was to overlord the team verbally; Reiss was to do most of the work. They had occasional falling outs, which would prove contagious. Five hundred strangers got together to help Humphrey, for the best part of a month, and, not surprisingly, frictions developed as toes were trod. People can be as mischievous as whales.

Krause and Reiss rigged the bridge with sound equipment. They put a hydrophone in the water to get the cetacean perspective. The tests were conducted during an incoming tide because the whale had gone under the bridge during an incoming tide. Sure enough, there was a high level of noise north of the span, and a low level south. Put another way, the whale had swum through the quiet side and would not return through the loud side. It was elementary. Traffic on the 270-foot lift bridge was spooking the beast.

Or maybe it was the giant shadow on the water.

Or the current from the power cable fastened to the deck.

Or none of the above.

Enter Dr. Kenneth Norris. He would become the gray eminence of the Humphrey operation. He is a marine mammalogist at the University of California, Santa Cruz. Peigin Barrett believes he is one of the nation's most respected cetacean scientists. He was brought in for retrospection when it became apparent that the whale was probably not going to go back to the ocean by himself, because of the Rio Vista Bridge, among other things, and might have to be urged in the right direction with something other than entreatments.

Norris was told that the whale had not responded to vessel guidance or the broadcast of predator (orca) sounds. He viewed that as distressing. He said the animal had to be turned from the fresh water as quickly as possible, and he suggested herding the creature with an Oriental manipulation known as the Oikomi method. Roughly translated, oikomi means to "chase into a corner." Dr. Norris said the idea is quite the same as using beaters to drive big game to a predestination, and the Japanese had used it successfully to school dolphins.

Norris explained that the beaters in the delta could be put on boats. They would then bang on hollow pipes stuck partway in the water. Done in unison, the pipes would create a chiming sound, instead of a cacophony of noise, and Humphrey might, underscore *might,* respond by moving away. Of course, he might also respond by moving toward the sound. Whales at sea are known to investigate everything from propeller noise to boat radios. Jack Findleton, for one, was cautious. Hitting pipes? There was only one ray of light: "We can have T-shirts made that say: 'We Banged for Humphrey!'"

Jack was game, though. As others, he had become convinced that something, anything, had to be done. He was further convinced that people like himself would have to do it. In that respect, the whale problem reminded him of Vietnam. The government was thus far befuddled and distant. Command was not to be confused with good purpose. The troops, therefore, were left to deal with the realities.

Let's be fair. The federal government was involved with Humphrey from the first sighting. One man from the National Marine Fisheries Service was on a monitoring boat in San Francisco Bay. A second joined him later. They were not authorities, however, or even administrators; Pete Chorney and Ed Jones were troops too, cops really, sent to enforce various laws that protect marine mammals.

The only serious government involvement in the first week was by the Coast Guard and, again, that's the rank and file. Besides, their presence was required. The Coast Guard is also charged with protecting marine mammals. They did a little more than that, though. They got emotionally involved and, by definition, became part of the solution. From time to time, they even stuck their necks over the edge of their orders.

One time the necks were attached to red faces. The Coast Guard allowed psychics aboard a monitoring boat. Psychics are people who believe they have paranormal perception and are susceptible to forces beyond the physical world. The group in question was from the New Frontiers Institute. Bear in mind that this is California; there is an organization in Berkeley that freezes clients when they die, so that they may be thawed out one fine day when advancing science permits.

Cherie Gierak is with the New Frontiers Institute. She and others told the Coast Guard they might be able to "send telepathic images to the whale." She said they would "work as a group mind," providing a "soothing, coaxing, guiding telepathy," the force of which would "push the animal to the sea." The Coast Guard says it seemed like a good idea at the time. Police departments occasionally use parapsychologists to solve crimes, with some apparent successes. Besides, as a sailor says, "we wuz desperate."

To be sure, Jack Findleton says, it was a weird sight: "I saw one of them standing on the bow of one of the small Coast Guard boats. He was up there like Moses on the Mount, arms outstretched. I thought he might have been the signalman, wanting to keep the boats on line, but he was trying to steer the whale, from fifty to sixty feet away, with his hands. I heard later that he was a soothsayer. I had to break up. They didn't influence Humphrey at all, and they didn't last very long. The Coast

Guard wouldn't let them back on board the second day, and no one that I know saw them again."

Most government agencies have acronyms, words formed by initials. CAB stands for Civil Aeronautics Board and EX-IM stands for the Export-Import Bank of the United States. COMCOGARDGRU is the mouthful used in place of Command Coast Guard River Group, the headquarters for the uniformed crews that participated in the Humphrey watch, and the National Marine Fisheries Service goes by the four letters NMFS, pronounced nymphs. All of this word brutalization is arbitrary, naturally, done because Noah Webster has passed on and can't fight back, so there will be a whimsical change in at least one acronym in this text: NMFS will be NMFiS; it reads better.

The fisheries service is a subsidiary of the National Oceanic and Atmospheric Administration (NOAA, pronounced NOAH, if you are getting the hang of this), which also monitors the weather. Brian Gorman, a spokesman, says NMFiS has a primary responsibility for researching and regulating ocean fishing within the two-hundred-mile economic boundary of America's coastlines. Other than this, the service has been ordered by Congress to enforce the provisions of the Marine Mammal Protection Act of 1972 and the Endangered Species Act of 1973, hence the participation in the errant whale dilemma.

Humphrey qualified on both counts. He was entitled to some government aid as a marine mammal and more as an endangered species. The marine mammal act is a statute of generalizations, but the endangered species act specifically ensures the protection of any genus (habitat included) thought to be depopulated to the extent that its existence is threatened. The penalty for violating the law can be as much as one year in jail, and a twenty-thousand-dollar fine. In 1985, the act protected a total of 877 birds, mammals, fish, crustaceans, plants, and insects, including eight species of the great whale: blue, bowhead, finback, gray, right, sei, sperm, and humpback.

There is, certainly, some difference between the whales and most of the other threatened creatures—not just structurally, either. The whale populations are comparatively large. NMFiS published a report in 1984, for instance, that indicated there were an estimated thirty-seven thousand to fifty-three thousand sei whales alive at the time and as many as one million sperms. Some of the smaller creatures, though, can be counted in double digits. In 1985, there were only twenty-seven California condors known in existence, only six in the wild. There were only thirty woodland caribou left, all in Idaho. Then there was the count of the dusky seaside sparrow, two remaining in Florida cages—both males.

The numbers aren't the whole story, however, except as they relate to percentage. There have never been very many dusky seaside sparrows, but there have, until recently, been plenty of whales. Farley Mowat says, in his book on Moby Joe, that there were almost five million great whales on earth before man started to hunt them intensively, and the population has been falling since. The Basques are supposed to have started the trend, introducing commercial whaling in the twelfth century. They also began the process of rendering the beasts at sea, but the world harvest remained relatively small until 1868, when a Norwegian named Svend Foyn invented the harpoon gun and sentenced whole nations of whales to death.

The gun introduced the era of modern whaling. The sport was gone completely and the slaughter was on. As many as eighty thousand were killed every year in the 1930s. Mowat says that twenty-five thousand finbacks were destroyed in 1956 alone, and that represented one-quarter of the family's population. In its entirety, the evidence suggests that as many as three of every four whales have been butchered over the centuries, and the estimated count today is thereby disquieting: apart from the sei and sperms, thirteen thousand to twenty thousand for the gray; three thousand to ten thousand for the blue; one hundred and five thousand for fins; five thousand to six thousand for the bowheads; and a mere three thousand to four thousand for the right whale.

As for humpbacks, there used to be at least three hundred thousand of them in the oceans. Now there are no more than seventy-five hundred to ten thousand worldwide, and only fifteen hundred to twenty-five hundred of them in the Pacific. When Humphrey wandered into the Sacramento River Delta, he was the last of a devastated tribe. The dead had been turned into lamp oil, corset stays, perfume stabilizers, dog food, glue, scrimshaw, and, when butter was reinvented, margarine. Of course, things are different today. We get corset stays from chemicals, and the great cetaceans are at last protected, by an international moratorium. However, we remain uncomfortable with past guilt. That may be one reason, if a subliminal one, that so many people put their oars in for Humphrey.

There was one serious deviation from the general sentiment for the whale up the river, or at least that's the report. A ranch hand may have taken a shot at the beast somewhere north of the Rio Vista Bridge. Ed Jones of NMFiS denies the story, and nothing was reported to any police station in the area, but at least three people say it happened.

One is Beverly Brownell. She lives on one of the ranches formed by the delta's dykes. Her husband manages the farm's agriculture and cattle business. She says she was "thrilled over and over" when the whale started coming her way, and so were most of the other women on the spread. The men were more reserved, she goes on, and one of them was hostile:

"That idiot took a shot at the poor thing. I know I shouldn't talk about it, but it didn't make any sense at all. My husband asked him why he did it, and he said he didn't know. He's kind of strange anyway. He's a bachelor and lives alone. I don't know when he did it, but I guess it would be in the evening. I don't think anyone else was there."

Two young men confirm Brownell's charge. One works on the ranch with the suspect, and the other fishes the area where the shooting is said to have taken place. Both testimonies are hearsay. The first man says he heard about the incident because the shooter "was supposed to have got in trouble." The second says he heard a shot from his boat.

That's all that's known for publication. Others on the ranch say nothing happened. If the shooting did take place, it might explain some things about the whale's behavior—why he kept going north, for one. If he was shot, and hit hard, he might have beat it from the fire zone and been afraid to return or he might have wandered around to wait for the healing.

It's impossible to say, but the theory is, at worst, as plausible as some of the other notions concerning Humphrey's mindset. Jim Hudnall, who represented something he called The Maui Whale Center, said the animal was crazy as a loon. Others thought openly that the whale may have come upriver to look for misplaced companions. No one will ever know, except maybe that flummoxed suspect with the rifle.

chapter four

JACK FINDLETON CAME BY HIS NEGATIVE OPINION OF GOVernment honestly enough, and the hard way other than that, so he may be forgiven if he sometimes turns the screws past the threads. Civil authority, he says in words to this effect, is not an exact science, and civil politics is a contradiction in terms. Chemists must study chemistry to get ahead, physicians should master medicine, but politicians can succeed merely by knowing their own interests.

Jack was not the only one objecting to the government's reticent involvement with the whale in the delta. Many of the volunteers were of a similar mind. The gripe in the beginning was that the government wasn't participating in a positive way and, later, when it was finally forced to participate, the critics said the bureaucracy was unforgivably disheveled, irresolute, faint of heart, and negligent.

The bulk of the complaints concerned NMFiS. That's natural because it had overall jurisdiction. Rio Vista had no authority. The counties along the waterways had very little. The state of California could have claimed the leadership but chose not to, and that left the federal fisheries service. Humphrey was protected by federal rules administered by federal agencies; that made it a federal whale.

The trouble was the federal responsibility was not clearly defined. If there is anything that throws the bureaucracy into a fit of inaction, it's the lack of precedent. Humphrey was the first cetacean of size in recent memory to be stuck up an American creek. He would set a modern world record for lingering in fresh water. NMFiS was obligated by law to protect the creature, but there was nothing in the books to mandate an active rescue.

The agency consequently kept its distance for as long as it could, and there were some legitimate reasons. One was the matter of, shall we say, animal rights. NMFiS officials were not certain that human beings should interfere with a whale in the wild. The humpback was in trouble, and going from bad to worse; yet NMFiS officials in Washington are pragmatists who associated with the bias of Brian Gibeson of the California Academy of Sciences. Dr. Gibeson said, "If the whale is dying, maybe we should just keep out of the way and let it."

Peigin Barrett of the California Marine Mammal Center thought that philosophy was rubbish, but she could afford to take the other side. She devotes her life to saving sealife, but she doesn't use tax money or answer to the voters. What's more, she may in the long pull be wasting her time. Men and woman cannot regulate the will of nature; it was the overriding power. The beasts of the wilderness have been getting into adversity, and sometimes out of it, since the first cell was divided. That is the violent wisdom of hill and dale, the survival of the fittest. People who accept it may serve the animal kingdom best.

Barrett rebuts, you can be sure. She says the beasts she rescues are very often injured by man. They are cut with propeller blades, poisoned by chemical wastes, or otherwise wounded by technology. She cites the case of a pregnant seal she once rescued that had been blinded by the blast of a shotgun. "We did it to them," she insists. "We can't let two of them die; our obligation is irrefutable."

She draws a parallel with Humphrey. The whale was not in the wild when it wandered up the Sacramento River Delta; it was corralled. It was fenced in by the bridges. It was imprisoned by human configurations on the waterway. The whale may have been frightened through the Golden Gate Bridge by a ship and, once inland, been threatened by man's clutter. The only conscionable thing to do was to lend assistance.

Still, the federal government delayed. In the civic arena, assistance is a synonym for money. The Coast Guard was already drawing from the budget; some of the consultants and monitors would also expect compensation. NMFiS is a relatively small agency. It operates with twelve hundred to fourteen hundred employees who absorb most of a $151 million budget. Nobody wanted to spend vital loose change to, great gods, rescue one whale.

For the first ten days of the humpback story, then, NMFiS stayed quiet and hoped for the best. The national director, Bill Gordon, was kept informed through field reports and news coverage. The regional director, Charlie Fullerton, was away on a fishing trip. No one, save the law enforcement officers, came to the river. The bitter joke in the delta was that fisheries officials only leave their desks for bodily functions.

Jack Findleton thinks, in the final analysis, that NMFiS was afraid to become fully involved, because, metaphorically, the waters in the Sacramento Delta were uncharted and crowded with dangerous shoals. "What if they [the authorities] came in, spent at lot of time and money, and failed? They would be the ones to catch the heat. They would be left to explain and stammer. They would have been forced to kiss the gunner's daughter, and then would have been tied to the cannon and lashed."

Despite extreme caution, the feds did make one commitment from the beginning. NMFiS officials in Washington said that if the whale had become dangerous to others, it would have had to have been destroyed. The delta was too thick with vessel traffic to take chances. Humphrey was more than large enough to overturn a powerboat or crush a skiff with its tail. In retrospect, the wonder is that it didn't, if only accidentally. If it had, the National Wildlife Service, which administers the Endangered Species Act, would have suspended the regulation for the public commonwealth.

NMFiS wouldn't have done the deed itself. The details would have been left to state or federal game wardens, and the scenario is purely speculation. NMFiS officers believe the whale would have been spared for anything, except a capital offense. The river could have been cleared for a time if the beast had merely gotten short, or threatening, but if someone had been killed, the response would have been a life for a life. The public would have turned against the cetacean under those conditions, and it would have been eliminated.

Charlie Fullerton of NMFiS says, for the record, that Humphrey "would have been protected" even if it turned murderous, but that is eyewash. Peigin Barrett was more devoted to the whale than Fullerton. She worked much harder for its welfare, but she says that if the beast had killed someone, she would have pulled her volunteers from the river and gone back to other things at CMMC. "There comes a time when one has to make hard choices," she explains. "I was willing to do anything to save the whale, so were all of the volunteers, but it would not have been worth the loss of a life."

The whale could have been destroyed in a variety of ways. Electrocution might have been considered, or big guns. But time might not have permitted the logistics necessary for the first, and the second could have been messy and risky in itself. The better way would have been to call eskimo hunters from Alaska. They have caught whales for subsistence since the beginning of their race. They use longboats, sometimes explosive harpoons, and renowned efficiency. They still use every part of the animal in the north, like the rest of us divide the remains of the cows that we slaughter: the blubber, the baleen, the hamburger, and the hides. Humphrey, the big fellow, was lovable, all right, and human in ways, but flipper pie is a delicacy in Point Barrow.

This is getting morbid, but the talk of the errant whale's demise is not ended. The government had one other plan from the outset. Peigin Barrett says NMFiS was convinced Humphrey had come upriver to die. Findleton says the agency was resigned to wait patiently until it did. California State Senator John Garamendi concludes that even when the feds were pressured into making a physical appearance in the delta, "they came basically to administer the last rites."

NMFiS made preliminaries by contacting people who were familiar with the rendering of whales, principally Dr. Gibeson, the man with the hard-nosed approach. Gibeson was known to have cut up other cetaceans, the largest of which had been an eighty-five-foot blue whale that had washed up on the Pacific Coast. Gibeson says it took several people four days to peel the flesh from the bones of that leviathan, and afterward the skeletal material was placed in a lot for public display.

Dr. Gibeson doesn't think Humphrey would have been put out for gandering. That would have been like stuffing Lassie's head, but he was prepared to strip the blubber from the humpback with long knives called flences, and to fill standing scientific orders for the stomach, the heart, the brain, and so on. Lawrence Livermore Laboratories in Los Angeles wanted a sample of Humphrey's sperm, for reasons never revealed, and they certainly weren't going to get it any other way than after the beast's untimely expiration.

There was another standing order from the world of science. The Moss Landing Marine Laboratory wanted a sample of the whale's feces. They sent a laid-back gentleman named Tom Kieckhefer to the Sacramento Delta to collect it. Jack Findleton says he "ran around with a butterfly net." Everyone laughed. In research, modesty is indubitably a vice.

By October 17, the whale had moved to a point more than sixty miles inland from the Pacific Ocean. It left the Sacramento Delta where that body turns sharply to the right, or east, and swam into water of the same size called Cache Slough, north by northwest now. The main channel was still twenty-five to fifty feet deep, but the salt content continued to shrink. The monitors were increasingly anxious to observe the whale's wanderings, therefore, so Jack loaded up that day with Mark and Debbie Ferrari, Bernie Krause, Diana Reiss, and Peigin Barrett. They found the animal "swirling" through the water not far from the Sacramento Deep Water Ship Channel.

"He was near the bank," Jack says, "and swirling is the best word I can use. He was mostly submerged, but shaking the surface. Debbie said that he might be going through a feeding pattern, which meant there should be a collection of food in the area. I turned on my depth finder to get a look at the bed of the river. The depth finder records the contours of the land. In this case, it showed that Humphrey was swimming in a large depression in the slough. Debbie got it right. That's where the small fish hang out.

"Debbie knew the business. So did most of the others. The thing was, they each had minds of their own, and that led to confusion. One would say the whale was tired, maybe, and another would say that was ridiculous. Sometimes I got caught in the middle. 'Move the boat closer, Jack.' 'No, don't get so damn close, Jack.' The arguments got to be an in-house joke. Everyone started calling the biologists the whale shrinks. Just lie quietly now and tell me your problems; hey, did you have difficulties with your father?

"But I learned. It was like classtime with Mr. Rogers. Humpbacks have two blow holes rather than one, but they are close together, and they don't blow water; it's steam that has been warmed inside their bodies. Their tails are known as the flukes. They are covered with barnacles that are also called white lice, and they are graceful things, a lot like butterfly wings. Debbie also showed me how to find Humphrey when he was submerged. She said she watched for his footprints, which are circles that he left on the surface of the water."

Another thing Jack learned was that whales, like people, can succumb to pressure. They do not like to be pushed too far. The whale shrinks used the term stress. Jack says it got to be exaggerated. "It was as if we were dealing with an eighty-thousand-pound child. Debbie would say, 'We are stressing it.' Mark would chime in that the 'stress level is too high.' Stress, stress, stress. I remember when [Coast Guard Lieutenant] John Carroll came up from San Francisco, he really got annoyed by the word. 'Look,' he said, 'the goddamned whale is not the only one here under stress.'"

Jack says the biologists needed reminding that the whale was, after all, only a whale. Yet they were never to accept the reproach. Debbie Ferrari would have brought all of Christiandom to pause, had she the way. She thought of the humpback in thaumaturgical terms. Diana Reiss used to know the late scientist Diane Fossey, who lived with the great apes of Africa for more than a decade. "The more you learn about the dignity of the gorilla," she said once, "the more you want to avoid people." Jack says Debbie is something like that with whales. "Nothing else counted. All she cared about was the humpback. I liked her. I never knew if she liked me."

Some of Debbie Ferrari's sentiment was apparently catching. Public interest in the whale burgeoned during the second week. Joyce Everett began printing and displaying hourly updates in the Little Darling's Bakery. Editor Walt Little ran eight-column headlines in Rio Vista's weekly newspaper, the *River News-Herald*. Jim Watson of Rio Vista's Bean Pot Restaurant said business was up thirty percent, and craftsmen in San Francisco wrote and recorded two musical ballads, "The Whale Rap," and "We Are The Whale," the lyrics of which were almost, not quite, as feebly considered as the arrangements.

Sports announcer Vin Scully talked of the creature during coverage of the World Series. Sally Downs sent a sweatshirt to Ronald Reagan. The California Marine Mammal Center received a thousand calls a day from all over the world, and the publicist for the National Oceanic and Atmospheric Administration, the parental bureau of NMFiS, wrote a departmental memo that said: "This critter has gotten more ink than all the fights over whaling in the last five years. There is nothing like a symbol. We should have named this thing Bambi."

Leana Anderson was thinking of naming it Brett, or something like that. She is a Sacramento hotel receptionist who wants to be a novelist. She says the Humphrey hoopla had all the elements of a, gasp, bodice-buster. "I thought about having two people volunteer to help in the rescue. Then they fall in love during the struggle. I guess it would be for Harlequin publishers. Of course, I don't know much about romance books. I usually read more serious literature. I like Stephen King very much. Did you see *The Firestarter?*"

Jack Findleton says the whale had more fans than Clint Eastwood. If it had died they would have dredged the river for suicides. An employee at the Rio Vista Justice Court was so impressed with the adventure that she compared it, kaf-kaf, to the discovery of America. "Four hundred and ninety-three years after Columbus landed in the new land," Sylvia Hutson noted, "another voyager set out in search of an unchartered world. Unlike Columbus, who discovered the earth was round, our humpback explorer discovered the [Sacramento River] Delta is relatively flat and it is not the place for a seagoing behemoth." Uh-huh, that's what she said.

Diana Del-Zampo of the Rio Vista Chamber of Commerce said it better. She is a short woman, but she is not built so low to the ground that things go over her head. She says when the whale first came up the river, her attitude was to "leave the damn thing alone." Then she says she fell in love with it "because it seemed to make everyone feel good."

Sorry, it's necessary to bring up the item again about whale poop. The subject warrants further discussion in another text. Okay, the collection attempt was a laugh. What was Tom Kieckhefer trying to find out, if Humphrey had piles? The fact is it might not have been a bad idea. One of the paramount scientific complaints during the visitation was that for all of the time spent with the mammal, and for all of the people involved, precious little physical intelligence was gathered. The whale may have learned more about the biologists than the biologists learned about the whale. No one truly knows to this day whether Humphrey was young or old, sick or well. Whale poop, at least, might have given some answers.

Diana Reiss says she lobbied to get a sample of the animal's skin. Jack wondered why divers were not sent into the water for a hands-on examination. Brian Gibeson points out that if a measure of blood had been extracted from the creature, a laborious, if painless, procedure on a beast of this size, the laboratory might have been able to verify the sex, draw conclusions about its health, and, with any luck, make a determination as to what the cetacean was doing so far from its own kind.

But, cuss, the feds would have no part of it. Debbie Ferrari didn't think the whale should be touched, and NMFiS followed her lead in laying down the law. Jack says NMFiS was afraid that if a medical examination was made, and the whale died, the agency would be blamed for provocation. Besides, the government position was that Humphrey was still a part of the infinite, as it were. He was not strictly speaking a specimen under observation, and he should be kept entirely free from instruments and other contaminations.

Stay tuned to that noble stand.

It will surface again, mockingly.

On October 18, Humphrey disappeared. He was sighted here and there, fleetingly, once near the deep water ship channel, then again in Cache Slough. Everyone was getting bored with the meandering. Some were getting fed up. The Coast Guard asked Bob Jones of NMFiS what it should do, and members say he replied by revealing he was going to withdraw for a while. The Coast Guard accepted that decision, and folded its own tents. It sent a message to COMCOGARDGRU, San Francisco, stating that the "whale's last known position was north of the

Rio Vista Bridge. This unit does not intend to dispatch vessels unless the situation significantly changes."

That left the whale without government protection, just before the one instance of shooting is said to have occurred. It also left the monitors to mull the remaining options. Jack recalls that another marine mammal was in the news at the time. Staff members from a California aquarium were moving a killer whale from Redwood City to San Francisco. Naturally it was on television. "It was a small thing. They just lifted it up in a sling. There was nothing to it, so people wondered why we were having such a time with Humphrey.

Jack was collared by suggestions on the street. The phones at CMMC rang off their cradles. Everyone had an idea at once. "God dang it," one man complained, "why don't you make a female whale out of papier-mâché, put a couple of sexy boobs on her, and lure the turkey out like that." A woman suggested throwing firecrackers at Humphrey. Another man said high-pressure hosing would work. The CMMC operators were advised, bing, bing, bing, to chain it to a barge, scare it with strobe lights, "stick it in the butt with a sharpened stick," and even drug it and drag it away.

Charlie Gregg of Rio Vista had a suggestion that made sense. He said that when he was a sailor, he used to see whales going into shallow water to scrape barnacles from their bottoms. He thought Humphrey might have the same worry, and would go back to the ocean if the excess baggage was removed. Barnacles are small crustaceans that attach themselves to underwater objects. Jack says the whale had them on his tail and on his head, but thanks to NMFiS no one got close enough to see if they were an underside problem.

Rio Vista's Diana Del-Zampo tells of one final public suggestion. She says she got a call at the Chamber of Commerce from a man who was impatiently convinced that he had the solution. He said all the biologists had to do was to chop a shark into little bits, put the mush in a perforated barrel, and coax the whale out with the fragrance. The man said whales eat sharks because they hate them, and the reason they hate them is that they are pests. He said two sharks will often force a whale to open its mouth, so a third can rush in and bite off its tongue. Del-Zampo says she could not help laughing at that, and the caller hung up.

Experts make mistakes too. Diana Reiss says that at one stage while Humphrey kept swimming north she found out he was going roughly in the direction of a Navy radio-transmitting station. The station broadcasts low-frequency communications to military ships in the Pacific, and Dr. Reiss thought the whale might be homed in on the electronics.

She asked the station attendants to turn the transmitters off, which they did, for two hours. Later, Reiss asked for a second interruption, and got a different response. The Navy command in San Francisco did not know about the first cutoff and was furious to find out about it. Low frequency ship communications are a primary piece of the nation's tripartite defense system. The Russians are coming, the Russians are coming, the Navy hollered; the fate of the free world can't be compromised for, sputter, what did you say it was, a *whale*?

The volunteers kept at it. The Coast Guard had left, so had the sheriff's patrols, and the federal government had barely arrived. Jack and the small team of biologists and specialists were the only ones still trying. They used the Delta Marina in Rio Vista as a headquarters. Jack had a slip and a charge account there. It is a nice spot—250 boating berths, a well-stocked ship's store, and the best restaurant in town. Sam Nichols is the harbor master.

Nichols is a man with large shoulders and a craggy face. He has thick hair, salt and pepper. He built his first boat when he was seventeen; he hasn't been away from the life since. He was forty-four during Humphrey. He donated dock space throughout the period, and lost money, but what the heck. He got miffed at one whale shrink, though. The man slept in a rental space at night, but was away at daybreak before the bill could be settled. "Hippylike fellow," Nichols says, "probably didn't know the first thing about boats."

Peigin Barrett sent a load of six-foot-long, cast-iron pipes to the marina. They were the tools Dr. Ken Norris had described when he suggested moving the whale with the Oikomi herding method. No one at the moment knew if any method would be used, but the volunteers experimented anyway. They filled the three-inch casings with water, taped the tops, and Dr. Reiss used a hydrophone to measure the decibels.

Dr. Reiss was thirty-seven then. She had long black hair and looked younger. She believes animals and humans can communicate, if they try. She has set up an experiment in an aquarium where dolphins are encouraged to trigger computer sounds to solicit items like balls and other playthings. Then they are encouraged to imitate the computer sounds to get the same results. The theory is that if the dolphins will associate sounds with items, humans can do the same thing and, after a while, two-way "conversation" will ensue.

"Beep" for ball, say.

"Grunt" for box.

And "#%*#*%" for you are stepping on my fin.

Where was the whale? Jack says the animal took the wrong turn at the confluence of Cache Slough and the Sacramento Deep Water Ship Channel. If it had gone up the channel, which runs straight as a priest for twenty miles, it would have been easier to follow. It would have been in deeper water too. The ship channel averages twenty-five feet. Cache Slough peters to ten or twelve feet, and connecting sloughs are so variable that they are not officially measured.

Another question: where was the state of California? Jack says the federal government took its lumps for its failure to act early in the whale dilemma, but the state recorded a worse performance almost without widespread censure. The state had a primary responsibility to protect boaters in the water, for example, and it had a moral and legal responsibility at least to assist in the protection of the mammal. The only active officer on the scene in the first two weeks, however, was a game warden named Jim Dixon, who lived in the Sacramento River Delta and offered his longtime knowledge of the region.

Jack says the governor, George Deukmejian, lived fifteen minutes away by helicopter, but did not put in a single appearance, nor did any of his principal aides or administrative officers. The state has a tax checkoff fund that may be used in cases of animal emergencies, but no one in charge was quick to make it or anything else available. One commentator guessed that the whale was a Democrat (Deukmejian is with the Grand Old Party). Others believe that Sacramento, like Washington, simply could not predict in the beginning that a whale would attract a rabid constituency of its own.

Eventually, State Senator John Garamendi would become the highest-ranking California official helping Humphrey. He is definitely a Democrat, and he says he only observed one occasion when Sacramento's "heavy hitters" took a look at the cetacean. He says several administrators from a couple of departments drove down in a state car one day: "One of them was from the Department of Resources, another was the director of Fish and Game. They got out of the car, walked around a little while, and asked a few questions. Then one of them said, 'Goddamned whale, anyway,' and they got back into the car and left."

Jack and the volunteer team searched for the whale all day on October 19—back and forth along the Sacramento River and Cache Slough. Then, late in the afternoon, a ranch hand named Richard Leverich called the Coast Guard to say he had "just seen the [naughty] thing." Leverich was excited, so much so that he gave incomplete directions. He said he noticed the whale "in the slough" while driving "over the bridge." When he hung up, the Coast Guard realized he had not said which slough or which bridge. A search was conducted. Calls went out. The service finally found Humphrey at what was essentially the end of the line. He had swum under the Liberty Island Bridge to the dead end of a finger of water known as Shag Slough.

Put simply, the beast could not have chosen a less desirable place. He did not like bridges anyway, he had already been trapped by the one at Rio Vista, and now this. Liberty Island Bridge is a stream crossing compared with Rio Vista. It is a tight one hundred feet wide, fifteen feet off the surface, and it is held up by cement pillars that are so close together they resemble baleen. Humphrey was bedamned. When members of the Coast Guard arrived, they said he swam to the bridge, turned around, and went to the end of the slough. The sailors said it was as if the whale was terrified.

Maybe it was. No one knew how Humphrey got to the end of Shag Slough, but few were willing to believe he swam there on purpose. The bridge is too much of an obstacle. The water is not inviting. The best conjecture the biologists could manage was that the animal went in by mistake. He may have swum north to the bridge in the evening, then turned around to go to sleep for the night. The tide could have picked up later, and Humphrey could have drifted through the bridge pilings with the current. He might also have scraped himself at the time, to use another sentence in the script, and that could account for his evident fear of the bridge.

Or, let's get it out, the whale could have been chased under the bridge with a rifle. Beverly Brownell says the man who may have shot at the beast lives near the Liberty Island Bridge, and it's easy to imagine another sequence of events. The whale swam north to the bridge, as the biologist believe, and it may also have stopped there to rest or sleep, but set aside the stuff about the tides. What if the animal was shot instead? If it was hit squarely, it could conceivably have been startled enough to charge through the pilings and it would be expected to remember the wounding and location.

The Coast Guard placed a boat on the south side of the bridge. The command also closed the slough to recreational use. When Jack arrived with the crew of biologists and technicians, they were not permitted on the other side of the bridge. It was just as well. Jack thinks Debbie Ferrari would have been overcome. No one could do anything whatsoever anyway. It was almost dusk. The sky was dark gray and that was fitting. Debbie looked like an accident victim. Peigin Barrett says the whole thing was melancholy. There was only one shred of promise, as Jack reconstructed it: "Now, by golly, the government was going to have to get involved."

chapter five

STATE SENATOR JOHN GARAMENDI IS THE ONLY PERSON WHO received a medal for trying to help Humphrey the Whale. He was given an award of merit by a grateful California conservation group. Some people grumbled that it was a setup; others argued that he deserved beatification. If there were no more pages in this narration, that would be a fair summation of the legislator's participation in the October 10, 1985 to November 4, 1985 events. Garamendi is a handsome, forty-year-old, well-to-do politician on the move. He would like to be governor. He would like to be anything on which the spotlight shines and the power collects. The result is he can't do very much, even something very nice, without sides being formed as to his motives and, quote, *designs,* end quote.

Oh the curses of handsome, forty-year-old politicians, and to some extent he deserves them. Critics say he is the kind of man who would succeed in small things if he were not so preoccupied with great ambitions. The problem is that he doesn't hide his light in a box. When Humphrey came to call, Garmendi had just dropped out of California's 1986 gubernatorial contest, but he kept his campaign office in business in the event something else opened up. What's more, he was one of only three state legislators who employed full-time press secretaries, and the others were the senate president and the speaker of the house. One of his colleagues says that "John is as humble as Job was irreverent." The road to gratification is often illuminated—in this instance harshly.

Still, Garamendi may not be so spiffily self-concerned as it appears, and when all is computed, Humphrey might not have made it without him. The senator likes to tell the story of how it all came about, he says he was urged into action by the fairy-tale advisement of his four-year-old daughter, how nice; once past the pap for the voters, he played a largely selfless, very demanding, politically perilous, and wholly central role in the whale adventure.

He started at the request of Mark and Debbie Ferrari, and under emergency conditions. When the whale ran out of waterway at Shag Slough, the Ferraris knew time was similarly drawing to a close. Furthermore, they knew the job at hand could no longer be left to a handful of civilian devotees. The federal government was not helping. The state was ignoring the case. Someone was needed who could push the buttons to get the lights on once and for all.

So, Garamendi. He lived in the Sacramento River Delta, he represented the region the whale was visiting, and he had a reputation for having clout. He was a Democrat in a Republican era, but he also enjoyed a scrap, and, as fate would have it, there was the daughter. "I knew about the whale, of course," Garamendi says. "So did my daughter, Merle. On the morning after it got stuck in Shag Slough, she came bouncing onto my bed. 'Daddy,' she said, 'what are you going to do about Humphrey the Whale?'"

Garamendi put his staff to work on the matter that day, and he began constructing a plan of action. He found out the state had a contingency fund, donated by cooperative taxpayers, that could be used to protect endangered animals. He also checked into the federal treasury, through Congressman Vic Fazio. He says he was told by the state that he could have twenty-five thousand dollars to help the whale, and he says Fazio, whose district includes part of the delta, promised to provide matching funds.

After that, Garamendi recruited commitments from county and other concerns, and tactfully. "I never scared anybody away with some kind of grand design," he explains. "I never said we were going to drive the whale all the way back to the Pacific Ocean. I said I just wanted to get it under the bridge at Liberty Island. I said we just might go from there and try Rio Vista Bridge. I emphasized that it was our *responsibility*. I said the whale had blundered behind prison bars. I said Liberty Bridge was our cell door."

In other words, the senator created a political structure that would force the federal and state governments to live up to their obligations. He arranged for the money. He helped arrange for volunteers to do the work and, along the way, he made a deal the authorities could not refuse—not without facing the mob, anyway. The ball was on the government's side of the net. Garamendi, and not, incidentally, his press spokesman, added pressure through the media.

It was a competent performance, and hazardous for a politican with grand dreams. The Ferraris say Garamendi placed his head on the block. "If things would have gone bad, John was the man at the microphones. He would have gotten the flak." As it was, the senator caught flak anyway. Republicans said he was posturing. Diana Del-Zampo says he was Napoleonic. He put his hand in the fire, and if he does become governor, if he becomes emperor, he may not again in his career accomplish so much for anyone as he did for Humphrey.

Diana Del-Zampo says that when Senator Garamendi began organizing the cooperative operation to save the whale, he ordered refreshments for the participants that included alcoholic spirits. Del-Zampo was asked to deliver the load, but when she did, she found that others in attendance thought the liquor was inappropriate. There were young people about. There were liability concerns. When she took the stuff back, and Garamendi found out, she says the Senator "waved his finger in my face, like he ruled the world we live in, and I never really thought much of him after that."

A fisherman who favors Shag Slough was irritated by the senator for a different reason. Dale Monk says the legislator "perpetuated" nonsense: "I'm sure everyone involved thought they were doing a hell of a thing, you know, reaching out to our brother the whale. That's a laugh. These things are always hypocritical. People will go out to save handsome birds caught in an oil slick, or cuddly seals being clubbed to death in Canada. What if the whale had been an ugly octopus or a wayward swarm of bees? We pick out causes with great care; no one is trying to save worm lizards."

The Coast Guard continued to block Shag Slough at Liberty Island Bridge. Jack and the technical team had to drive to the area by car. They were not pleased with what they saw. The waterway, which runs due north from Cache Slough, resembles a large irrigation ditch, which in fact it is in some measure, and it serves as one of the boundaries of an oblong, six-thousand-acre island. The island was created fifty years ago, during an active period of delta reclamation, and has been used since then as a cattle ranch and farm.

Cows grazed a few hundred feet from Humphrey. Ripe milo grew beyond the twenty-foot levees. There was a migrant labor camp, a post office, and a ranch headquarters just as close. Bev Brownell, the business manager for the ranch, said the whale chose an inopportune moment to call. Toxic fertilizers and pesticides had just been flushed into the slough. Moreover, it was harvest time. The people who were coming to see the whale were causing traffic jams on a single access road, and they were interfering with business.

The Ferraris didn't care about business, of course. The only thing of concern was what they called "this beautiful animal." They were distressed by its plight. The whale was, in a figure of speech, entombed in water that was only fifteen to twenty feet deep, one hundred feet wide, a mile in length, and maybe entombed is not a figure of speech at that. Humphrey swam in circles at the far north end, and made only hasty inspection trips to the dreaded bridge. There were shallows all around, and two turbid tributaries which led to nowhere.

Bob Jones, the sole NMFiS representative, let it be known he thought the odyssey was over. Men at the ranch said the critter was dead and didn't know it. The volunteer team was also pessimistic. Peigin Barrett found out there was no salt in the water, only poison. Debbie Ferrari said Humphrey's skin was definitely beginning to sluff. Diane Reiss said there did not seem to be any noise around the small bridge, so the animal was evidently avoiding it for personal reasons. Jack says he could have hung a hook on the gloom.

"Debbie started crying on my one side. Peigin started on the other. I got the feeling they were giving up with Bob Jones, so I got a little angry at that. All right, they were the biologists, the technicians, the whole nine yards, but I made a seat-of-the-pants decision. I said, hey darlin's, I don't know if the animal is sick or not, and I don't know how we're going to get it to get up and go, but the whale is still breathing; it's still going strong. We're going to get this thing out of here; trust me, we'll do it."

The state responded rapidly to John Garamendi's call for cooperation, not overwhelmingly, but at least rapidly. John Passerello, the governor's representative from California's Office of Emergency Services, was assigned to Rio Vista. He was not assigned by the governor, as his title suggests; he was dispatched in line with his normal duties. He was the fellow in the state who tried to line up federal funding for state emergencies; thus he would play two parts in the Humphrey affair. He would provide some state assistance and he would labor to get Uncle Sam to pay the resulting bills.

He proceeded gingerly. Caution serves the man with empty pockets. He says he had some money at his disposal for natural disasters, "but this was not a natural disaster," and he did not think Garamendi could get hold of the money he promised. He says he likes the senator. He stayed at the legislator's home in Walnut Grove on some nights of the operation. "I knew the state wasn't going to give John any money, and that left Washington, D.C. I set out to convince the federal government that the whale was federal property, and when I did that, I no longer had to worry about debts."

Passerello told Garamendi that his agency was on board, and as tangible evidence, he offered the use of a contingent from the California Conservation Corps (CCC). Passerello was one of the early organizers of the corps, which is a clone of the federal agency that operated during the Great Depression. The original CCC was peopled by five hundred thousand unemployed men who were put to work on conservation and resource development projects throughout the country; the California version has two thousand disadvantaged men and women (ages eighteen to twenty-three) who do similar work. By 1985, Passerelo said they had fought forest fires and mudslides and planted fifteen million trees.

Passerello also offered the services of his wife, Beverly. She works for the Office of Emergency Services as a full-time volunteer. She says there are thirteen hundred of her members in the state, working free in such capacities as doctoring the needy and holding back floods. She says volunteers can't fill positions that are normally occupied by paid workers; that keeps them from being a threat to the bureaucratic gentry. She says she works ten hours a day for OES, as a legislative liaison, and she would be handling logistics for the Humphrey rescue.

The Passerellos were one of several husband and wife teams in the effort. The Ferraris have been mentioned. Game Warden Jim Dixon's wife, Kristin, made a lasting contribution, and John Garamendi's wife, Pattie, pitched in intermittently. There were a pair of volunteers from Sacramento named Mike and Becky Pulsipher, also Bob and Bonnie Lenz, and two mariners named Jim and Sandy Cook. Sally Downs is closely associated with volunteer Dick Whitesides. Scottish-born volunteer Patrick Johnson has a similar relationship with CMMC member Deidre McCarthy, and one of Jack Findleton's boat commanders, Chuck Walker, invited his wife, Jean, to share the duties one afternoon, whereupon she proved to be a blonde and bouncy addition to this whale rescue family tree.

Jim Dixon says it was as if almost everyone in California came out to see the whale in Shag Slough. The news media reported that the whale had now ventured seventy-five miles from the Pacific Ocean. That's close to the distance between New York and Philadelphia, and this was one of the only times in memory when the largest animal in recorded history could be seen from a few feet away while it carried on in its natural environment.

People arrived by the hundreds, then thousands. Police were summoned to direct traffic. A bait shop in Rio Vista sold mimeographed roadmaps for a dollar each. Everyone was kept on the west side of the slough, between the bridge and the north end, and the animal was never more than a football field away. Sometimes it came so close to the levees that spectators could see the scars on its hump. When it threw steam from its blowholes, there was applause of appreciation.

Merchants sold food and souvenirs. Some of the designed sweat shirts were twenty-five dollars. Conservationists worked the banks for solicitations and support. One man from Greenpeace encountered a skeptic, and the following exchange is reported: "What is Greenpeace?"
"We work for the rights of whales."
"What about other animals?"
"We believe in protecting them too."
"You people, you're all so young."
"I'm twenty-seven."
"Christ. I'll bet you don't remember Trigger."
"Who?"

"Trigger."

"What was that?"

"See, I told you. It was the Lone Ranger's horse."

Dixon was asked to help keep control. The road to the area was barricaded in the evening, and no one was allowed after dark. "One night a woman drove up, and I had to tell her it was off limits. She said she had driven all the way from Sausalito, and could I at least tell her how Humphrey was doing. I said the last I knew he was doing all right. She said, 'Thank you. Now I can go back home in peace.' Then she said, 'Oh, gosh, how do I get back to Sausalito?'"

John Garamendi finally got everyone together at meetings in Rio Vista on Wednesday, October 23. The issue was about to be joined. The federal government delegated James Lecky and Sheridan Stone from the NMFiS regional office in Los Angeles. The state was technically absent, but John Passerello was on his way to enlist. Drs. Reiss and Krause were there. So were Peigin Barrett and the Ferraris. Kay Woodson attended for Congressman Fazio, an area businessman named Bill Dutra participated, and Jack Findleton sat in for the plebeians, at least at the end of the proceedings. Added together, there were twenty-five officials, scientists, conservationists, and amalgamated volunteers getting down to it.

There was not much negative discussion. The principals had made their decisions earlier to move from monitoring the whale to helping it. NMFiS agreed to pick up the bills, which precipitated state cooperation, and the volunteers had been ready to go for a few days short of two weeks. The purpose of the meeting was to divide areas of responsibility, decide on a course of action, and begin. The clock was ticking. Debbie Ferrari said the whale was deteriorating in Shag Slough. Authorities had been contacted across the United States, and the unanimous reply was that death was imminent.

Rescue ideas were discussed one by one. Kay Woodson wrote them down on yellow legal paper. She is a woman who hangs on to her elbows during conversation, and she had worked for Vic Fazio for three months. Fazio represents California's Fourth Congressional District, from Sacramento to Vallejo, and from the Sacramento River to the edge of the national forests. The district is heavily Democratic, fortunately for Fazio, who is a liberal legislator. He served in the California Assembly before taking a relatively obscure seat in Congress in 1978, when it was prudently vacated by an incumbent who was found to be maintaining two families.

Kay Woodson wrote, "Sonic harassment, False Magnetic Field, Bubble Curtain, Large Sling, and Seal Bomb Detonation (last resort)." None of the suggestions washed. The Ferraris said they would not tolerate harassment, or—"are you crazy?"—detonations. The false magnetic field sounded like Star Wars and, as for the large sling, enough said. The only feasible idea was the one Ken Norris had offered a week before, the Oikomi method, banging pipes in the water. They would be put on a fleet of boats, hammered by volunteers, and maybe the wrongway whale would get the message.

The operation was on. Jim Lecky, a biologist, inherited command by dint of his federal position, but Garamendi, a politico, would shepherd the administration. Lecky pushed papers for a living; he was not prepared to lead a pioneering activation. He told reporters that he didn't have any sentiment for the whale: "It's an animal with me, he said. "It's not an emotional issue." He also said that, all in all, he would rather be home in Los Angeles. Garamendi says graciously that the NMFiS executive "did a good job under the circumstance," but the circumstance was that he was as much out of his element as was Humphrey.

Here's how the rest of the organizational chart was constructed. Peigin would be in charge of CMMC volunteers. The Ferraris would be scientific liaisons. Beverly Passerello would handle food and equipment. Bernie Krause was to direct the water operation, and NMFiS asked Jack to admiral the fleet of boats, quite a promotion for the old E-5. The operation headquarters was established at Dutra Construction Company, Bill Dutra's family firm; it specializes in heavy marine excavation, and it's one of the concerns that helped reclaim and shape the Sacramento River Delta.

One more note on the organizational session. Jack missed a lot of it to check out a thought at Shag Slough. What was Humphrey so afraid of at Liberty Island Bridge? No one knew then that he might have been a target of a shooting. The whale shrinks clung to the guess that he was injured passing through. That meant there might be something else in the water at the bridge, submerged and unseen. Jack took his boat to get a better look; he went on both sides of the bridge and mapped the bed underneath with his depth finder.

He got to the meeting late. He stood in the wings for a time, and then caught Debbie's eye. She asked what he was up to, and he said he thought he had something interesting. He showed the group two rolls of paper from his fathom machine. "See here," he said, pointing with a pencil, "there is debris all along the water under the bridge. It's probably branches and wood that has collected in snags."

That wasn't all. The graph paper showed there were broken pilings sticking up in the water. They were obviously the leftovers from when the bridge was made of wood. They were jagged, and some of them were sharp, and they may have given the unwary and hapless Humphrey a whale of a good scratch.

Jack put the data in safekeeping.

It would be most useful later.

Bingo, as Jack would say. Everything had come together like filings on a magnet. The feds were in, the state was in, and private industry as well had agreed to lend a wrench or two in the unique undertaking. But let it be known again that there was one group prepared all along to roll up its sleeves: the volunteers. "Bless them," says Bill Gordon, who was the director of the National Marine Fisheries Service when Humphrey got lost. Gordon says NMFiS systematically relies on people who donate their skills and energies to conservation projects, and, he continues, "the delta whale operation could not have been established without them."

Most of the volunteers were delivered by the California Marine Mammal Center. Peigin Barrett had made arrangements for 150 members to stand by from the fifth day of the whale's sojourn. She says virtually all of those contacted had full-time occupations, but many of the employers were also sympathetic to the troubled Mysticeti, and, on signal, the volunteers left their offices, factories, and schools to take up duties as gofers, factotums, and roustabouts at Rio Vista.

Mary Jo Schramm. She takes care of public relations at CMMC, and she fielded press inquiries in the delta. She works for a construction consulting firm. That's when she's not wrestling with marine life for CMMC. "We all volunteer one day a week at the center," she says. "Don't ask why. The work just has a way of dominating your outlook. I can tell you how to take down a 250-pound elephant seal. You throw a blanket over its eyes, to blind it, then straddle its shoulders when its head comes up. Then get someone to help."

Patrick Johnson. He is from Scotland. He was a gamekeeper there and he says the things in *Lady Chatterly's Lover* aren't true. He met an American tourist in Ireland a few years ago and came with her to California. She is Deirdre McCarthy. They were engaged when Humphrey was wandering. They're both members of CMMC. "I was not overly confident about the whale rescue," Johnson says. "I didn't get my hopes up. I was on one of the standby boats at first. We waited a lot for something to happen at Shag Slough. We fished, mostly. Quite honestly, it got a little boring."

Mary Sanders. At sixty-eight, she was the oldest volunteer. She was born two years before women were allowed to vote in this country. She was in the Woman's Army Corps during World War II, rising from an enlisted woman to the rank of captain. She became an attorney when the fighting stopped, before becoming a law librarian in San Francisco. She ran errands in Rio Vista, she worked on a chase boat, she slept in an Army Reserve barracks, and she notes: "We were there to get the whale out, as long as it took. In rescues, you have to keep trying."

Starr Light. She is a dental hygienist and says her father had a way with words. Her middle initial is *E*. She made many of the initial calls to set up the volunteer contingent. Then she worked in the Humphrey communications center in Rio Vista. She drove back and forth each day from the Coast, because she had a sick cat at home, and she estimates she got three hours of sleep a night. "I lined up about half of the CMMC volunteers. They came in from all over. Of course, not one of them asked for a penny in return."

The CMMC facility occupies an abandoned Nike missile base on the northern side of the Golden Gate Bridge. The center overlooks the Pacific Ocean there and what are called the Marian Headlands. Peigin Barrett had been executive director for eight years in 1985. She had three paid assistants and nine thousand contributing members. Two hundred members volunteer time. They pick up strays and nurse the sick to health. Barrett says that sixty-five percent of the volunteers are women, the average age is twenty-six to thirty-five years, and on an average count, they rescue and nurse 140 animals a year. "Some people don't believe they can make a difference." Barrett says. "It's obvious at CMMC that they can and do."

The marine mammal center didn't provide all of the volunteers. People in Rio Vista also helped pull on the rope. The business groups at the river port pitched in as well. Diana Del-Zampo opened the Chamber of Commerce office to the whale junkies, and Main Street merchants contributed everything from hardware to refreshments, especially refreshments.

Del-Zampo was asked to cook the food. She was used to preparing food for the multitudes. She is the chef for the community's annual crabfest, boiling crustaceans for five hundred guests; there are raves all the way back to Italy. She required ingredients, though, so she asked merchants to give until it hurt for Humphrey, now almost the town's holy relic.

Del-Zampo was born and raised in the area. She wears small earrings and a Delta River Rat T-shirt. She says she knew the merchants would come through. Little Darling's Bakery contributed pastries; the Delta Deli made sandwiches; Do Quick Supermarket gave ham; and Ernie's Restaurant, fried chicken. A total of thirty-two local concerns and people made donations.

Del-Zampo prepared two or three meals a day, for as many as 150 people, and she didn't mind at all, except once. That was when Senator Garamendi decided that the press should be fed. The volunteers thought the media could fend for itself. Kay Woodson took the food to the reporters that day, and, "Do you know what? They had the gall to ask me to go get seconds."

Jack readied eight boats on the night before the whale rescue began. He had two of his own, three given by Dutra Construction; the rest belonged to friends. One friend was Barry Canevero. He is a forty-three-year-old Italian who gave up selling and repairing household appliances in the delta because it was aggravating his heart condition. He became a charterboat captain instead. Jack calls him the best fisherman on the Sacramento River, and he was to serve, unofficially anyway, as second in command of the Save Humphrey Flotilla.

Jack drove to Sacramento from Rio Vista that night. He had to fetch two boat skippers, and say goodbye for some time to his wife, Olive. She thought he should stay and get some sleep, but he was anxious to get back, and that's a fair summation of the relationship. They were married the year before Humphrey. She is slender and quiet; he is burly and deafening. She is reserved; he is raring to go. They live in a modest development house, where Jack insists the phone be answered with the name of his business, Sacramento Sport Fishing Guides.

Olive Findleton has a degree in home economics from Sacramento State College. She doesn't remember a course in humoring husbands who fish for a living. She worked for the state when Humphrey swallowed her spouse, investigating complaints for the Office of Equal Employment Opportunity. She says she went to see Humphrey once. She says she was "really impressed," though she hesitates to use transitive verbs, particularly following an adverb. After that, she received regular progress reports from Jack, who is Popeye to this Olive.

When Jack got back to Rio Vista, he found he had a dead battery in one of his boats. There was no place open to get it fixed. He was the captain of the fleet, dead in the water already, until the police came to the rescue of the rescuer, with a battery charger. The boats in the flotilla were numbered one through eight for formation and radio identification. The call signal would be *Whale*. Jack was Whale One. P.J. Glavin was the skipper of Whale Two, Chuck Walker was Whale Three, Mark Jacoby was Whale Four, Paul Caselon was Whale Five, Dick Whitesides was Whale Six, Barry Canevero was Whale Seven. Bob and Bonnie Lenz were Whale Eight.

Jack finally got to bed in the early morning. He kept a pickup truck at the Delta Marina and he bunked there. Barry Canevero says that when the supreme commander snored, he blew the tailgate from the vehicle, but Jack says he hardly slept at all. "I kept working on the plan for the following day. I had to lay out the boating maneuvers. I drew Xs and Os in a notebook, like the coach of the Jets, and then I drew Os and Xs. I was very nervous. It was like a night before a mission in that goddamned Vietnam. I didn't have to worry about getting hurt, however; or, when you think about it, with an eighty-thousand-pound whale, maybe I did."

Can we say the whale couldn't sleep much either? We can't, but there was evidence that it was somewhat restless. Peigin Barrett was assigned a twenty-four-hour watch at Shag Slough.

Tom Kieckhefer of the Moss Landing Marine Laboratory and volunteer Linda Calhoun reported the following observations: Humphrey swam clockwise upstream and counterclockwise by the bridge. The whale showed its fluke infrequently, but reacted to noise on the levees. Sometimes, it tried to squeeze into one of the two shallow tributaries that continued from the end of the slough into the farmlands.

The animal also made sounds. Kieckhefer says it grunted at wide intervals, and a woman named Janice Covello says it bayed in the night. She lives on the Liberty Island ranch, and went out in the evenings, when the crowds had gone, to watch the whale. She says it would swim in circles and then bellow. "That's the best way to describe it. It was a bellow. I mean, you could tell he didn't like it in there."

chapter six

NOTHING IS SO GOOD AS IT SEEMS BEFORE IT HAPPENS, AS George Eliot testified, so there were great expectations when the participants collected on the first official day of Operation Whale Rescue. It was October 24, shortly before eight in the morning. The boats were mustered at the Delta Marina, and some time was spent loading equipment and people. Jack says he took four volunteers and technicians on his Bayliner, and four people were also selected to crew each of the other vessels. The weather was agreeable, the sun was in view, and the boats proceeded in single file into the Sacramento River and north, fourteen nautical miles to Shag Slough.

Jack Findleton, especially, was sailing on anticipation. There was no guarantee the operation would succeed, indeed there were good reasons to conclude it would not, but he leans to the opinion that anxiety destroys initiative, and that there is no good purpose in raising umbrellas before it rains. He says he had "fat hopes," though, he admits, no experience. He took the lead of the procession, setting a smart pace. Dr. Bernie Krause and Debbie Ferarri were on the boat. He also had two volunteers aboard, Mike Pulsipher, a Sacramento businessman with an interest in marine biology and Tom Haidet, a member of the California Marine Mammal Center.

Jack had some concerns about the new people. There were two dozen volunteers who had not been on the water with the whale before, and he didn't know how they would react. The whale was one thing when viewed from the security of the riverbank, but quite another when seen close up. It was twice as long as any of the boats in the operation that A. M. It was nearly as big as a basketball court is wide, and Jack told all hands that when it turned in the water, and moved toward one of the crews, it would have the look and the menace of a U-Boat. He told everyone to be calm, and use discretion. Neither people nor craft should be jeopardized.

"I emphasized safety over and over. I told everybody it was the priority importance. I didn't want anyone getting hurt. I knew the boat skippers understood, because I knew they had experience on the water, but I worried some about the new volunteers. I told them to follow orders, and keep their eyes open. I said we were out there to help the whale, not to la-de-da. They seemed like good people, and I didn't think Peigin Barrett would bring in ringers, but I still had to be a little like Captain Bligh. I didn't know for sure, but I had a definite feeling that if something bad happened, I would be the one hung out to dry."

Jack was also troubled that Barry Canevero was not on line the first day. He says the Italian is one of the most reliable watermen in the Sacramento River Delta, but he was recruited late to the operation and Bernie Krause would not put him immediately on the first team. Krause said the boats had already been numbered and integrated with marked strips of tape, and he did not want to change things around at the last minute. Jack argued, but lost. Krause had administrative command of the boats. Jack says Krause was not even on the water most of the time. He was off on his regular work every other day, and some animosity developed.

There was a good deal of animosity, actually, between various people. No one came to blows, but arguments and differences festered throughout the rescue activity. Several of the leading characters in the drama threatened to quit at one time or another. The state finally did quit, and at a critical moment. Jack says this is what Coast Guard Lieutenant John Carroll meant when he said that people in the operation were under as much stress as the whale. To be sure, the participants handled the enmities as quietly as could be expected, but beware the fury of patient people. Operation Whale Rescue succeeded because of a balance of antagonisms.

Lieutenant Carroll stopped the teams of boats at an island at the entrance to Shag Slough. He told Jack that he would be in charge of safety and law enforcement during the rescue attempt, and he would start by inspecting each vessel in the flotilla. He was thirty-two years old, based in San Francisco, where he lived on an eighty-two-foot Norwegian trawler in China Basin. He was professional, taciturn, dashing in his starched white uniform, and he fell in love with one of the volunteers on the operation.

The lieutenant checked registrations, life preservers, signal devices, and spark arresters, where applicable. He found one defect, and a minor grumble followed. Patrick Johnson, the Scottish volunteer, had a life preserver that wasn't acceptable. Carroll says it looked as if it had gone through the Civil War and every farmer shot at it. Johnson said he thought it was dumb. "Forgawdsakes, everybody out there was trying to be a big shot." The incident was settled when Lieutenant Carroll offered a new Coast Guard preserver.

The officer then explained the rules of engagement. He said Jack would be in charge of the boat maneuvers, but if anything took place regarding safety, the Coast Guard would take control. He said that if a boat sunk, or someone fell overboard, the other boats should stay out of the way. Everyone would naturally want to help, but that could lead to complications. He had two divers and three paramedics on his boat who would handle any incident.

As another precaution, Lieutenant Carroll sent the following message to mariners from San Francisco Bay to Cache Slough: "The National Marine Fisheries Service, in conjunction with other federal, state and local law enforcement agencies, will commence an operation to escort the disoriented whale from Shag Slough...To assure the maximum success possible, all mariners are requested to stay away from the area of the operation, consisting of six to eight vessels, as it moves toward the sea. The National Marine Fisheries Service advises that anyone within two thousand yards of the whale will endanger the rescue and may be subject to civil or criminal penalties."

State and local authorities were also on guard. They cleared the road along Shag Slough of outside spectators. Only the participants and the media were allowed. Everyone on shore was cautioned to be quiet. The whale might react to any sound, and that could foul the water operation. The reporters were told that the consensus of the scientific opinion that had been gathered was that the whale was weakening, and had only two or three more days to live.

Sure enough, the whale did appear to be slowing down. Volunteers on watch had noticed that it was swimming slower and breathing less often. More ominously, it was also having reactions to the brackish water. Jack says the color of its hide had changed from dark to light. Debbie Ferrari said skin was flaking off. Some others said the critter may have been discolored by algae or stains in the slough, but Ferrari insisted the tissue was now waterlogged.

John Passerello brought a hundred members of the California Conservation Corps to the shores of the slough. They were to be used if and when Humphrey was driven back under the bridge. Passerello got several large sheets of sturdy polyethylene and rolled them up in a row along the south railing of the bridge, where he secured the edges to supporting posts.

Says Passerello, "We didn't know if we could get the whale through or not, but we thought we should be ready if we did. We didn't want him to swim under the bridge going south, and then come back going north, so the CCC people were to throw the plastic over the railing when the whale went through, and it would hang there to block the whale's return."

Good idea, Jack says. But it meant that the kids would have to get on the bridge, and that meant they could be at risk. The whale was almost half as long as the concrete structure, and it was probably its equal in weight. Jack asked for everyone to be removed from the bridge. He assumed that his request was heeded, and he didn't have time later to check.

The final spadework was the coordination of radio communications. That was another of John Carroll's duties. All of the boats, except one, had very high frequency radios and, in that case, Citizen's Band (CB) equipment was used. Otherwise, the Coast Guard lieutenant assigned the following VHF numbers: Channel 6 for system control among all whale boats on the water, Channel 81 for communications with the shore command, and Channels 22 and 23 between the Coast Guard and law enforcement only.

All federal regulations and restrictions were to apply, including proper identification and proper language. Jack says both were forgotten in the shuffle. Lieutenant Carroll told the crews that in view of the complexity of the job to be done, "absolutely no unauthorized chatter can be tolerated. All VHF transmissions will be restricted to essential instructions and replies, and the use of hollering is encouraged as an alternative means of passing messages between boats."

Jack says he took the fleet of boats under Liberty Island Bridge at mid-morning, one by one. "I was first, followed by the Coast Guard vessel, followed by even-numbered boats and then odd-numbered boats. That means there were six on the line, or five when John Carroll pulled out and anchored on the west bank. The other boats were skippered by P.J. Glavin, Chuck Walker, Mark Jacoby, and Paul Caselon. That's as many boats as I thought I needed north of the bridge. I left three boats downwater in the slough to act as reserves."

Jack used his boat to edge around the cetacean and block the larger of the tributaries at the dead end of the slough. As instructed, the volunteers on the other boats began banging on their Oikomi pipes. One pipe was strapped to each boat. Each was filled three-quarters of the way with water, capped on one end and taped shut on the other. The beaters used hammers that had been purchased for between fifteen and twenty-eight dollars. The ones for twenty-eight dollars, no surprise, were bought by the federal government. The ringing was in unison.

"And it worked," Jack says.

It was outstanding. We had practiced beating on the pipes a couple of nights earlier, but we didn't know what to expect. As soon as we hit them in the slough, the whale responded. If we hit them on one side of him, he'd turn the other way. If we hit them on the other, he'd turn back. Dave Carrick was on one of the boats. He's a friend of mine from Sacramento. When the whale started to move to the bridge, he thought it was going to be easy. We were all optimistic. We seemed to be finally in control.

I brought the boats around according to the plan I had worked out. Basically, we formed a semicircle with Humphrey between us and the bridge. P.J. Glavin and Mark

Jacoby were on my left, facing south; Paul Caselon and Chuck Walker were to the right. We were well spread out at first. I didn't want to push the whale too much to start with. We also went very slow. We adjusted our speed to the animal's. I confess I was very nervous. Everything was going good. Maybe it was too good; yup, turned out that it was.

When the whale got to the bridge, maybe ten to fifteen feet away, he turned right. I can't say I blamed him. There are twenty-six poles that support the bridge, thirteen to a side, and they are no more than twelve to fifteen feet apart. From his perspective, it must have looked like the teeth of a comb. He was at least ten feet wide himself, and he had those gigantic pectoral flippers. Outstretched, he was as wide as he was long. He was like a railroad car in the water, and he let us know early that he wasn't going to try to squeeze through that bridge.

I had the boats back off then. Debbie Ferrari did not want to get the animal ruffled, but we were just getting started. At least we were forcing him to confront the bridge. We backed up, and then we started ringing the pipes again. I remember Debbie said to do it all together, on count, every ten seconds, but there had to be a few deviations. We would push the whale to the bridge. Then he would turn around to come back at us, and everyone started screaming: "Beat the damn pipes; beat those pipes!"

You see, none of us knew what the whale was going to do. It was conceivable that he would charge, or just knock us aside as a nuisance, so we banged for all we were worth. I kept making certain that everyone was alert and paying attention to what we were doing. Some of the volunteers aboard had a professional interest in Humphrey. They were students, or conservationists, and things of that nature. I caught one of them dropping his hammer one time to pick up a camera; I had to tell him to either get back to work or get off the boat.

Johnny Carson's writers were among those following the bombilations in Shag Slough, and the television comedian mentioned the rescue operation in one of his late-night monologues. He said people in the boats were trying to maneuver the animal by banging on pipes in the water. The whale didn't seem to mind, but the state of California was wondering what to do with ten thousand deaf guppies.

Mark Ferrari had another odd view of the Humphrey activity. He cruised over Shag Slough in a helicopter. He thought he would be able to see the whale better from the air, and prevent it from hiding from the fleet. It became evident, however, as Joe Louis said of an opponent, that "the beast could run but not hide." The slough was too small, too shallow, and Ferrari would be relegated to ground duty thereafter.

He may have preferred that. He kept close to the mass media. He became the most quoted individual on the operation. The press queried him on everything from personal philosophy to biological calculations. He was identified as a cetologist. He was said to have taken thirty-six thousand photographs of whales, and at Shag Slough, he was professionally deliberate. "It's a longshot," he told scribbling reporters, with sangfroid.

Mark Ferrari's prognosis was in tune with the first day's events in Shag Slough. Despite the control the boat crews exerted with their presence and the pipe sounds, it became obvious the whale still had options of its own. Debbie Ferrari kept warning Jack to keep a distance, to minimize pressure, and he, in turn, ordered the boats to stay loose. The crews were successful to a point, which was the whale's congress with the Liberty Bridge; they would herd him to the structure, stop at his insistence, retreat to let him breathe, but as the day passed, a pattern of futility developed.

That failure came into focus in the early afternoon, when Humphrey swam to shallow water on the east side of the span and beached himself. Debbie said, "oh no." Jack said, "Jumping Jesus." Dave Carrick said it wasn't going to be so easy after all. The great creature had been stranded in ten feet of water at Decker Island; now he had five feet tops. Jack says Humphrey kept his head under water, but the rest of him was bare as the side of a barn. The fisherman looked at the sky. Debbie looked at her feet, and everyone else looked at Humphrey strung out under a lone eucalyptus tree.

Debbie was upset. She brought up her favorite word again. Whenever something went wrong, and the whale didn't re-

spond as predicted, she said it was under stress. It was "stressed out." It was "stressing out." I never knew what that meant, exactly, or why it was such a terrible condition. She talked like it was horrid, however, as if the whale would throw a fit, or hold its breath until it died, I don't know. "Jack," she said, repeatedly, "the whale is stressed out," or "it can't take the stress," or "we have to reduce the stress factor," or, once: "It's just stressed to the limit."

My own opinion was that the whale was very canny. He went to the beach because he knew that would scare us away. It had happened several times before Shag Slough. We'd get close to the animal, to monitor it, but then when it moved toward the shore, we would get nervous and pull off, same thing at Liberty Island Bridge. We pushed it, then it got tired, and, lo and behold, it went to the bank. It think it just wanted to rest for a while. I think that it knew that we would stop what we were doing if it bumped the ground, and we would let him the hell alone for a little while.

Advantage Humphrey, then. Jack ordered the boats to idle at dead stop while the whale worked itself free from the mud. It was not all the way over the shoal, so it was not seriously stuck. Dave Carrick was in the boat closest to that edge of the bridge, and he says the big thing churned up earth and water, and was floating in five minutes. Debbie voted soon after for a recess of one hour. Bernie Krause and officials on the levees concurred. Jack pulled the fleet back to the middle of the slough, giving Humphrey a quarter mile to himself, and team leaders debated to death.

Peigin Barrett was not in a boat, but she needed the time-out too. She watched the operation from the top of the bridge, where she lent body language to the tumult and shouting. She leaned this way when the whale got close to the span, and she leaned that way when he shrank from the assignment. She told friends she was shaking—only fools are never frightened—but she also knew, with James Russell Lowell, that the misfortunes that are hardest to bear are those which never come. Besides, she believes in miracles.

She is Irish Catholic. The name Peigin is lifted from a Gaelic term of endearment. When she was a child growing up in Connecticut, she had an allergic reaction to animals. That was a drag, because she loved everything in the forest and sea. The allergy was connected to asthma, so the doctors lacked hope, but her mother told her to recite a novena to Saint Jude, the patron saint of hopeless cases. Barrett says she made the entreatment every day for years, and when she was thirteen, right hand to God, "the reaction stopped and I was cured."

Now Barrett is a patron saint in her own right. Well, she's a beneficent guardian of pinnipeds and cetaceans anyway. She did not start the California Marine Mammal Center, but she took over its direction shortly after its origination in 1975. It was then and remains today the only voluntary concern of its kind in the nation. The center rescued its first mammal from tapeworms; it was a sea lion named Herman. He is one of at least fourteen hundred finned creatures who have since been treated at the mammal center and returned to nature.

Barrett is in her forties. She has a poster on her office wall that says she is wanted, dead or alive, for everything including "impaired herring." And she's never forgotten the lesson of Saint Jude. Just before Humphrey came into the delta, she finished an informal study course on miracles, and her conclusion is that they are the rule rather than the exception in life, for faithful believers at least. "Miracles are not magical," she says. "They are the result of people sharing what is really possible. If everyone had thought Humphrey the whale was just a dead fish in the river, he would have been. We saved it because we were positive."

There was time for light assessment during the pause in the effort at Shag Slough. Lieutenant Carroll of the Coast Guard recognized that Humphrey was not the only difficulty of the day. Radio communication was as sore as after surgery. The channels were overused, the give and take was garbled, and people who didn't have anything to do with the operation were butting in and out with suggestions and wisecracks: "Listen up, listen up. I just saw the whale in my swimming pool."

Jack says he couldn't reach the ground command on any frequency, and the single boat with CB equipment was a full-scale pain in the aft. The FCC monitored the frequencies throughout the mission, listening for four-letter words, and one time, telling P.J. Glavin to get his transmitter repaired. After some hours, Jack felt like giving the whole system a bath, and began to rely increasingly on waves and sign language.

As things went, the FCC forgave the intemperate phraseology, but it did issue one citation during the operation. The sheriff of Costra County called Sally Downs of Rio Vista while the rescue was underway, and he used an illegal channel. That was not exactly a hanging felony, and for the sheriff, it was nothing at all, but Downs was notified that if she was found guilty for her part in the despicable erratum, she would be liable for a ten-thousand-dollar fine.

We are at home with the preposterous.

Chuck Walker sat behind the wheel of Whale Three, reposing like Buddha on a break. He was thirty-three years old, five-foot four, and all of two hundred pounds. One of the volunteers said he looked like he had muscles in places where other people don't even have places. He was one of three boat skippers borrowed from the Dutra Construction Company, P.J. Glavin and Paul Caselon the others. Walker works with the Dutra barge crews. They put in seawalls, pier pilings, and they repair leaks in the levees. One associate says that when the pile drivers have difficulties with pilings, he has the impression that "if Chuck would just get up on the pole, and start stomping, the lumber wouldn't dare resist."

Walker says he had one Dutra hand with him on his boat, Jesse Santos, and two volunteers from CMMC: Jan Roletto, the center's curator, and Kathy Mulvany. He says he was not used to working with women on the water, but he managed. "For one thing, I didn't bring any food for them, and nobody else brought any. I understood someone was going to send lunches to the boats, and maybe soft drinks, but we didn't get anything. I saw that people on the levees were eating, and I heard the press even got food, but no one bothered with the boat crews. I thought that was an insult. We were doing the work. Everybody else could get something in a cafe, or go to a hamburger stand, but we were stuck in the boats."

Such is the fate of the working class. Walker says the people in the whale boats were ignored in a litany of ways. He says the newspaper and television reporters flocked to John Garamendi, Jim Lecky, Mark Ferrari, and others who organized the rescue, neglecting the men and women who got the calluses. "There was only one time the reporters talked to me," Walker goes on. "That was one night when I was docking my boat at Delta Marina. The TV people had a big spotlight shining at my boat. I asked them to turn it off so I could tie up, but they didn't. Then they stuck a microphone in my face, and somebody asked me where the whale was. I told him, and that was it. The lights went out, and they left. One time."

One of the people most interested in the Shag Slough operation was seventy miles away in another county. Esther Malcolm, age ninety-one, read about Humphrey in the newspapers, heard about him on radio, and "prayed for him every day." She says she felt a kinship with the creature. He was, after all, wandering around in what used to be her backyard.

Mrs. Malcolm's husband, Robert, created Liberty Island in the early part of the century. He was a rancher and planter, and hired clamshell dredges to reclaim the land from the marshes. Clamshell dredges are barges equipped with booms and buckets that move earth from here to there; they were invented for the specific purpose of building levees.

Mrs. Malcolm says it took years to isolate the land from the water. "And it was simply wonderful to see it made." She wrote a small history of the construction, which is in a special library collection at the University of California, Davis. She lived in a retirement home in 1985, where she says she participated in the Humphrey rescue in spirit.

The whale boat maneuvers resumed in the afternoon. Jack used hand signals to supplement the disorderly VHF communications. Otherwise, the procedures were the same as before. The boats moved in the shape of a bow, the volunteers beat the Oikomi pipes, and Debbie Ferrari kept watch for stress. Jack wanted to tighten the boat formation, to apply greater influence, but the biologist wouldn't have it. The pattern of the morning was repeated: the Mysticeti was herded easily to the bridge, where it stopped short of the pilings, turned around, and forced the operation to retreat in kind.

Jack, as they say, was befuddled, but he was also inspired. The whale was no longer just a mountain of buoyant blubber; he was thinking, reasonable, and rational. Jack says it was "damn near like he was human". He moved on a predictable course. He advertised his preferences and limitations, and he was every bit the same as the fat kid on the block, as someone thought later, "who can't make it over the fence, so he wanders in circles, breathless, sulking, a mite embarrassed, wondering what is the big fuss anyway."

Fat kid, indeed. Mark Ferrari said Humphrey was as large as "ten Indian elephants, or 525 people smushed together," and he repeated that it had enormous intelligence to boot. The whale's brain is not as big as it might be; it is actually one of the smallest in the animal kingdom when measured against body dimensions; yet it is decidedly one of the most serviceable. Scientists say the brain of a great whale is about the size of a rolled-up mattress. It has the same composition as a human brain or, for that matter, a cat brain or a dog brain, and it is constructed of the recognizable parts which control movements and thinking.

As for intelligence, the whale is said to be about as smart as a pig. That's not bad; pigs are among the most intelligent animals on earth, but the comparison seems to indicate that size is relative. Dr. R.J. Hofman, a scientist with the Marine Mammal Commission of the United States, says people should be careful when considering cetacean intellect. Whales sing, they communicate with each other, they plot to catch food for sustenance, but human they are not. Humphrey did not have the brainpower of John Garamendi's precocious, four-year-old daughter.

He was not smart enough to give reliable signals about his physical condition, for instance. The bond he established with his rescuers fell short of actual discovery. Debbie Ferrari thought he looked sluggish in the Sacramento River, and then thought he looked worse in Shag Slough, but the whale was incapable of verification. She says the animals often mask their symptoms: "You can't really tell sometimes if they are sick or well. They don't go to bed and take aspirins like we do. They may look all right one day, and then the next day they can turn over and die."

That's one reason Ferrari was reluctant to prod the animal

too much. The stress was not just a factor of psychology. The biologists and specialists thought that if Humphrey was indeed as tuckered as he appeared, then provoking him would have been piling on. Stress might have aggravated the physical problems, and the whale might not have looked or acted differently until he died. Ferrari knew that Jack thought she was too timid, that she was too concerned by half, but she would not put the whale between Scylla and Charybdis.

After the whale boats tried eight or nine times to nudge Humphrey under the bridge, without success, Ferrari said enough was enough. She conferred with Jack, with Bernie Krause, and with others on shore, and the concordance was to call it a day.

Jay Ziegler relayed the news to the press contingent on shore. He was Senator Garamendi's twenty-three-year-old press secretary, and like everyone else in the operation, he was winging it. He had worked for a radio station and a television station. He knew something about arranging interviews for Garamendi, but he had never been in the eye of a news storm. He says there were thirty reporters to deal with on a slow day, and a hundred for events such as Shag Slough; there were also continuing calls from the foreign media: "Wo ist der Walfisch?"

Ziegler says he had two responsibilities. One was to the news, the other was to the mission, and they were neatly compatible. "I tried to tell everything that was going on, so the reporters could do their jobs, and I also tried to keep them coming back for more. We had to keep the story alive. We had to keep the national and international interest. That was what dictated the tenure of the operation. If the press had left, or if the world wasn't listening and watching, the federal government might have just walked away."

Ziegler held nightly press conferences. Garamendi was usually available, and the state and federal officials were on call and relatively candid. One problem was that there were only three public telephones in all of Rio Vista, the same as saying for miles around. Ziegler solved the bummer by setting up a mobile communications center for the press, complete with free phones, compliments of John Garamendi, the man who was campaigning for (fill in the blank).

The principals of the operation held a meeting that evening to put together the next move. The debate started from the premise that the whale and the bridge were incompatible, like Visigoths and virgins. Senator Garamendi was convinced that the structure over Shag Slough was the cetacean's Maginot Line. The whale was not going to go through it, he argued, any other way than in pieces, and therefore the solution was to tear the blasted thing out of the water.

The senator said he had already contacted the requisite officials about that option, and he had been told that the bridge was due to be replaced anyway, probably within a year. He said officers of the California Department of Transportation advised him that if it meant the difference between the whale's living and dying, they would be willing to start the job immediately. He said the engineers believed that, in view of the emergency, the pilings could be removed in twenty-four to forty-eight hours.

Garamendi said there was at least one tangential consideration. The farmhands at Liberty Island were conducting a harvest, and the managers were concerned about further disruption. The milo had to be taken from one side of the slough to the other, to get to market, and there was only one bridge. Garamendi said the ranch would cooperate, however, if the federal government would spring for the cost of a hundred acres of milo. The senator said that would amount to four thousand dollars.

Jim Lecky of the National Marine Fisheries Service started to perspire. The bill for the whale operation had already escalated beyond projected figures. Besides, some biologists wondered what the dismantling of the bridge would do to Humphrey. The work would be noisy, maybe explosive, and go on around the clock. Here's the word again: stress. The animal shouldn't be killed to save it.

But did anyone have a better idea? Yes. Jack Findleton did. He had found out that the spaces between the bridge pilings were cluttered with bramble and other debris, and that could be the cause of Humphrey's fears. Whales are not so nearsighted as popularly thought, and no animal would willingly mosey through an arabesque. Jack's depth-finder pictures were passed around, for all to see, and the vote was to clean out the mess for the second day.

Jack slept in the back of his pickup again. He may have been promoted to admiral, but the accommodations were still rank and file. He was not so nervous anymore, however, and he had to get some sleep, so he brought in one luxury item. He put a sleeping bag over the truck bed, so he wouldn't feel the ribs in the floor. Posh. The word was invented when wealthy Englishmen used to travel by ship from India to England and did not want the heat of the sun in their cabins, so they ordered port side accommodations out and starboard home.

> Oh, the rare old Whale, mid storm and gale,
>   In his ocean home will be
> A giant in might, where might is right,
>   But lame if he leaves the sea.

chapter seven

Dutra Construction sent one of its barges to Shag Slough early in the morning of October 25. The work crews used a boom and hook to grapple with the debris under the Liberty Island Bridge. They pulled out what was described as a "shutbag" of branches, driftwood, siding boards, tumbleweed, and, so the rumor went, one or two pairs of feminine undergarments. They did not have the equipment to yank the truncated pilings, but when Jack mapped the area after sunup, he was satisfied that at least half of the garbage had been cleared from the bed of the bridge overall, and more was taken from the crucial tenth and eleventh supports.

Jack clustered the whale boats at an irrigation pumphouse downwater from the bridge. There had been loading delays at Delta Marina and it was already ten o'clock. That didn't matter, though, because the tide was out. It would have been temerarious to start the operation without sufficient water. The whale had enough difficulty with the bridge without being expected to crawl through it in mud. Still, everyone was impatient. Impulse is the fuel that replaces reason when the juices start to flow. Jack says the administrators on the beach began gesturing at the boats and grousing over the radios: "Come on, out there. Let's go. Get it in gear."

Happily, the radio calls were at least disciplined. John Carroll of the Coast Guard had worked with the participants the evening before, explaining that *this* is the transmitter and *that* is the receiver, and suggesting kindly that Tryon Edwards was ten-four when he wrote that "common sense is, of all kinds, the most uncommon, because it implies discretion." Carroll said each call should be preceded by call signals, taking care not to butt into another conversation, and that users should speak clearly, succinctly, without undue haste, and, if there is still trouble with the broadcasting, it might be prudent to just forget the radio, get out, and wave.

Jack says there were several personnel changes the second day in the slough. Dr. Krause could not attend because of a previous occupational assignment, so Tom Haidet of the California Marine Mammal Center filled his administrative role on the water. More importantly, Jack put a sixth boat on the first team. Barry Canevero was called from a standby slot. Jack thought the ruddy-faced charter-boat captain would add smoke, fire, and experience to the herding effort, not to mention considerable shoulder. He had a twenty-six-foot vessel, *Fishing Fool III,* and that would give Humphrey one more inducement to do what he was told.

There was another reason Jack wanted Canevero. He is a fellow in the California Striped Bass Association. Jack is serious about his prejudices. God made man, and then he made striped bass to lend interest. Jack says the association is organized to encourage the conservation and propagation of the fish. It has brought about the cleanup of some habitats and contributed to the regulations that govern size limits and daily catches. Jack flew the organizational flag in the first day's effort, so did Mark Jacoby in Whale Boat Four. Now Barry would be showing the colors too, for the cameras; without ventilation, a cause is merely a hobby.

Jack says Mark Ferrari had come down from the helicopter and would watch the day's events from the levee. Sheridan Stone of the National Marine Fisheries Service was there with him, as was John Garamendi, Jay Ziegler, and others of the administrative staff. Peigin Barrett of CMMC was with Dr. Diana Reiss, who was conducting soundings from a small dock on the southwest side of the bridge. Time passed to 11 A.M., and the impatience grew into restlessness.

"Jack, when are you going to begin?"

"Are we on a time schedule, darlin'?"

Findleton still had to wait for good water. Bugger the mates on shore. "I was calling the shots from the water. I wasn't going to be influenced to do something wrong. Besides, I think one reason they got so itchy was that they were losing faith. I don't think they thought we could do it anymore."

Dr. Ken Norris of the University of California was also on the bank. He was asked to fly in because the operation was thought to be at a critical moment, and he agreed with that conclusion. He told the participants that there was not enough food in the slough for the whale, and there was no salt. The whale had two options, therefore: "He can stay here and die shortly, or he can get out and have a chance."

Jack told his boat crews that they would proceed in the same manner as the day before, with three early exceptions. There would be six boats on line instead of five. That would tighten the semicircle a little, and the objective would be to direct the whale generally to the west side of the bridge, and specifically between the tenth and eleventh supporting poles. The pilings were numbered left to right on the bridge, looking south, or east to west, from shallow water to deep.

Jack says he believes the whale must have come up the slough through poles ten and eleven, give or take a piling to the east side. That is the place where the bridge rises highest in the air, about twenty feet at mean tide, and it's the place where the water runs the deepest, also about twenty feet with a favorable tide. The depth was cut somewhat by the bramble and old pilings, but it seemed to be sufficient.

Of course, what constituted sufficiency in this regard was an unknown. The whale might not go under the bridge even if there were no pilings or entanglements at all. He hadn't gone back between the supports at the Rio Vista Bridge, and they were fifty instead of twenty feet apart. What's more, there was the possibility that Humphrey's hesitation was more psychological than physical. If he had been shot at the bridge, or otherwise wounded, he might never again confront the source of the pain.

Jack says the low morale he sensed on the shore was a wounding of its own kind. He had been told by some of the volunteers that the rescue had become a throw of dice with no markings. He continued to feel, however, with Ahab and everyone else who has faced a whale in its domain, that positive conviction was a helpful tool.

We started before noon. The tide still wouldn't be high for a couple of hours, but the people on the bank kept hollering.

I think the press was also getting on edge, not that I cared especially.

We did it according to memory. We slipped into the slough, waiting for the whale to surface, and then we cruised into the half circle behind him. The pipe ringers were clanging away. Everything was just as it had been. Humphrey turned from the north end and obediently swam before us to the bridge. The old smoothy, he knew the moves by now. I could hear him thinking: "Hey, here we go again, this is kind of fun, except at the goddamned bridge. If they get too close, I'm just gonna scare the heck out of them."

Lo and behold, he did. When we got him to the bridge, he turned counterclockwise, over to the west bank where he beached himself the previous day. I was ready this time. I wasn't going to let him start using Debbie Ferrari right away. I sent Whale Four to head him off, and then wait there, in the low water, to prevent him from making the threats. Mark Jacoby was still in boat four. He had his father, Jake, with him. I think that was the only father-son team on the Humphrey Operation.

I suppose at that time they were in a tight spot. If the whale was determined to get to that beach, he could have gone right through the Jacobys, but they kept the position. The whale came at them a number of times, and things got a little tense, they only had a 16-foot boat. Did I say a little tense. That is like saying a little pregnant. Everybody was wound up. We wanted to get going. I was guilty too. I kept a strong hand. I don't think I was nasty, but I didn't want any flagging, any deviation, and I was very vocal about it.

Jack says the whale seemed to be in the same condition that it had been on day one. He says the animal continued to turn from black to gray, owing to freshwater osmosis, and it was less than rambunctious. When he had seen it in the Sacramento River, it moved at double time and rolled with deliberate suavity. Now it plodded, albeit not blindly. "Tighten up boat three," Jack yelled. "P.J., come on around." Humphrey swam in circles, doing only what he wished, and not one thing more.

P.J. Glavin was not as used to taking orders as he was to giving them. He was twenty-seven, but a topkick. He started working for Dutra Construction when he was nineteen and now supervised twenty-two flatdeck barges, five bigger rigs, and a pair of tugboats. Still, he followed Jack's demands, and he had more things on his mind than arguing about them, the water for one. No wonder the whale was losing its skin. Shag Slough was so polluted with chemicals that if anyone had fallen overboard, he would have decayed before he drowned.

Jake Jacoby had no trouble with the orders either. He was retired from both the United States Army and the California Highway Patrol. He was a compact man who wore a white goatee and looked vaguely like Colonel Sanders. His son, Mark, sold mobile homes in Sacramento. There was one other Jacoby on the boat, Jake's grandson, John Riley. The fourth member of the crew was Victoria Knight, a CMMC volunteer over from the coast.

Jake said Victoria personified the people from the marine mammal center. She was in her late teens, wore no makeup, and was studying to be a stockbroker. She was willing to work, was anything but boisterous, and was agreeably absorbed with the mission. Jake says that Victoria did not waste a lot of time on conversation, but on the morning of the second day she said: "Do you realize we may be making history here?" Jake replied, "I guess."

Jack and the boats kept trying, and the whale was now allowed less and less space. He was blocked on the east side of the bridge by the Jacobys. He did not seem to like the west side, because that's where most of the supporting staff congregated, so he turned in smaller circles, twelve o'clock to nine o'clock to six o'clock to three. Usually all the animal showed of himself was his hump. He brought his tail from the water once or twice, but never his head. Consequently, he had to go fairly long periods without breathing.

How?

The answer is that whales, like people, and most other vertebrates, have protective reflexes when they go under water and, in their case, the reflexes permit longer durations. The average human being can submerge for between thirty and sixty seconds, and the world's record is said to be about fourteen minutes, but that is nothing for cetaceans. Humphrey dived for fifteen minutes or more. Had he been of a mind, he might have been able to stay down twice that long. One species, the sperm whale, has been clocked underwater for two hours.

Basically, the whales do it as do humans. They probably hyperventilate for long dives; in other words, they take a lot of deep breaths, because that supplants the carbon dioxide in their blood with oxygen. Then when they go under, their reflexes take over. Their breathing is shut off automatically, their heart slows to conserve energy, and their body tissue begins to metabolize larger amounts of carbohydrates, so that the cells won't be left without essential nourishment and fuel.

Of course, the whale has one obvious advantage in the process. It has barrels rather than pints of blood, hence an enormous oxygen reserve. It also has a system that tolerates great amounts of toxic carbon dioxide. Finally, whales are not ultimately forced to breathe, as are humans, and so there is no danger of their running out of time and ingesting water. They can run out of time, to be sure, and do if they are trapped underwater. When this happens, they will not drown, as will people; they expire from suffocation.

The tide was still rising at 1:00 P.M.. Jack thought it was time to get the humpback breathing a little faster. The boat maneuvers had failed again and again, and Jack said he wanted to do something to break the everlasting pattern:

The silly thing had been swimming around in front of us for two hours, not to mention the seven hours the day before, and so I felt we had to tighten up even more. Everybody worried about stress; I wanted to interject some stress.

So we started to inch up on him. It was like, very slow. He had paused at the middle of the bridge, and we brought the boats closer than they had ever been. We didn't let up when he moved a little toward the bridge, either. I was no more than a hundred feet away. The lead boats were on my port; the starboard boats were even closer. Everything was very quiet. Everyone on the shore was looking down. At that point, I may have been holding my breath longer than Humphrey.

Then, all I can say is that it just got angry. It rolled over on its side and slapped the water with one of those fifteen-foot-long pectoral fins. I think it was a slap heard round the world. There were a hundred newspeople on the bank, and everyone recorded it on cameras or on tape. The photographs were reproduced everywhere from the East Coast papers to the local six o'clock news. Humphrey certainly knew how to get our attention. Water splashed twenty feet in the air.

The thing is, it was completely unexpected. The fellow had been a milquetoast for two full weeks, but now we got a glimpse of another side. It had the power to mow us down like minnows. It didn't move forward or back; it just turned over on its side, lifted that goddamned flipper up like the trunk of a tree, and hit the water several times. Slap, slap, slap! It must have sent waves all the way to the river.

Jack says he turned immediately to Debbie Ferrari. She was looking around the cabin and was not completely surprised.

"Why'd he do that?" Jack asked.

"It's a sign of anger," she said.

"What's next?" Jack continued.

She said it might breach.

Breach? That's what Moby Dick did when he pulverized the longboats from the *Pequod*. The leap of the great whale is the most bellicose and spectacular movement in the animal community. If Humphrey jumped, and if something got in the way—a man, a boat, even the bridge—it would be crushed. Jack says he didn't linger over Ferrari's message. He got on the horn and hollered, "Get back, everybody back, two hundred yards." When they did, they decided, wisely, to stay there.

The whale stayed in place too. John Garamendi says the beast blew out a large explosion of air and sank like a meteor to the bottom of Shag Slough. Senator Garamendi was standing on the bridge, looking over the railing, and his blood drained toward his footwear. When the water smoothed over, there were a few popping bubbles, and the legislator thought it was like a last sigh: "I said, God, is it dead?"

Ken Norris was standing next to Garamendi. He has seen more marine animals than Garamendi has used campaign adjectives, and he understands them somewhat better. He said, "Don't worry. It's not dead, it's just sulking. The whale is like a little kid who doesn't want to go to bed. He gets angry when he doesn't get his own way. I don't think we are being as firm with him as we should be."

Garamendi consulted with his aides and other administrators. He drew the same conclusion that he had argued the night before: the bridge at Liberty Island was a locked gate. He left the slough then, drove back to the operation headquarters in Rio Vista, and, costs notwithstanding, began making dispositions with state engineers to tear the span down.

Lunch on the water was also miscarried that afternoon. Beverly Passerello arranged to have fast-food delivered to the boat crews, and it turned out to be hamburgers. "A" hamburger "apiece," as Jack recollects. P.J. Glavin says they were bone dry, Mark Jacoby says they were without lettuce or pickles, and Jack adds they were unaccompanied by anything to drink: "zero water and zero soda pop."

Passerello says it wasn't her fault. She put in the order, but had no quality control. "We didn't pay for any of the food. All of it was donated. We got some from merchants in Rio Vista; we got some from McDonalds and Burger King. Some of those places were thirty to forty miles from the boat operation, and we couldn't really be choosy. We got two hundred hamburgers in Benicia one day, and couldn't even find the boats."

Sure sure.

> There was a young man on the water,
> Who thereafter decided he oughta,
> Bring his own lunch
> And share with the bunch
> And to hell with what Beverly had broughta.

Peigin Barrett and Diana Reiss had watched the early afternoon activity from a small platform that reaches out over the water on the freedom side of the bridge. Barrett was dejected by the continuing failures, and perfectly funereal over the whale's hysterics before lunch. Reiss, however, is a research scientist and was absorbed more in the technicalities of what was going on. She had put a hydrophone in the slough and was taping sounds from the subsurface.

Some of the sounds were out of the ordinary. At one point she taped impulses that suggested the whale may have sonar, or at least the animal equivalent of sonar. She thinks she detected signals that shot from the whale, bounced off objects in the water, and returned to the whale. Submarines use electronic sound waves in this way to navigate in the seas, and some marine creatures also have the capability.

The sonar is called echo location as it relates to animals. Dr. Reiss's findings were believed to be important because humpbacks had not been known to use the system. Reiss says she was surprised to get the suggestion on tape; it sounded like the turning of a ratchet when Humphrey got close to the bridge. She says she turned the tapes over to Dr. Norris for confirmation, which has not been forthcoming.

Norris and his students have examined the data at the mammalogy laboratory at the University of California, Santa Cruz, and have not been able to find a connection between the sounds and sonar. Norris told Reiss that he could not say for sure if she heard echo relocation or not, but he had educated doubts. As of 1986, Humphrey and his colleagues were still officially thought to be guided only by sight, sound, and sensitive hides.

Just before 3:00 P.M. the team leaders held a somber meeting on the west levee. Jack pulled his boat from the line to attend, but told Barry Canevero to maintain the rest of the formation so the whale wouldn't swim back to the north end of the slough, a goal that was doubtless on its mind. The opinion was the whale had tired of the contention of the last days. Cetaceans are animals who do not mix with people all of their lives, if they are lucky, and are not pursued by boats unless they are being hunted. Humphrey must have been grossly troubled by the sound of the motors, the ring of the pipes, the shadows of the crowds, and Jack: "Whale Five, this is Whale One. Did you say you wanted a potty break?"

Jack says Ken Norris, Mark and Debbie Ferrari, Peigin Barrett, Jim Dixon, et al., were on the bank, scratching their shoulders, wiping their faces with their hands, disagreeing as to what course of action should be taken. Debbie said Humphrey might get angry each time the boats came at him now. Dr. Norris added that the whale may be using psychology as a defense; the mammalogist said that if the whale knew he could send everyone running by slapping his tail, or making other retaliations, he would do it, and if the rescue operation accepted the conditioning it would be paralyzed.

Game Warden Dixon picked up on the Norris warning. He thought all along that the whale would have to be bullied for its own good. Bears that come out of the mountains to forage in backyard garbage cans have to be hogtied and forced back or they will be destroyed. Dogs who wander into the streets have to be restrained before they are struck by traffic. Dixon did not want to antagonize the whale any more than necessary, but he believed that if the options came down to harassing the creature or letting it die slowly in Shag Slough, there was only one responsible choice.

Peigin Barrett said that was all well and good, but what if the harassment killed the whale? She was another one who worried about the consequence of stress, and she noted that everyone on the operation was in love with Humphrey.

"So you love the whale," Dixon said.

Barrett said she did.

"Well, maybe you love him too much."

Tons of words for an ounce of wisdom. Jack says he agreed completely with Dr. Norris: "He was right; Humphrey was conditioning us, which is like saying he was outsmarting us, and that got me. I liked Humphrey too. I got the feeling he liked me, but I wasn't going to let him get my number. I talked with John Carroll about the tides. He said the water was as high as it was going to get. At about 3:30 P.M., I decided I wasn't going to wait around anymore while everyone talked. I decided to get back on my boat and do whatever was necessary to drive that big sucker under the bridge."

On the water, Jack conferred with Barry Canevero and his crew. The crew included Sam Mallory, another charter-boat captain, and two volunteers from the California Marine Mammal Center. Jack said he was going to abandon the failed method of trying to herd the whale with a half circle of boats. The time had come for direct action. All of the boats would be kept in formation, as an intimidation, and two of the boats would move out of the formation to actually push the beast. Jack said one boat would be his and the other, Canevero's.

The operation would therefore be more dangerous. There is small choice in bad fruit. Fleas must sometimes feast on the lips of lions. Jack told Canevero's crew that the whale was capable of murder. He did not want to minimize the risk. He said the crew would be risking its life." Then he said that if anyone wanted to leave, speak up. One volunteer from CMMC accepted the offer and was taken to shore by the Coast Guard.

The whale made a sudden rush among the remaining tangles of the other lines; by so doing, irresistibly dragged the more involved boats of Stubb and Flask towards his flukes; dashed them together like two rolling husks on a surf-beaten beach, and then, diving down into the sea, disappeared in a coiling maelstrom, in which, for a space, the odorous cedar chips of the wreckage danced about and round, like the grated nutmeg in a swiftly stirred bowl of punch. (Moby Dick)

Jack also advised his own crew of the peril. Debbie Ferrari, Mike Pulsipher, and Tom Haidet wanted to see it through. He told them to stay down for the duration, sit or kneel; the only ones who would be up and around would be Canevero and himself. Both boats had cabins. That wasn't much against eighty thousand pounds, but it was something. As extra preparation, Jack put government sounding devices on the chase vessels. Each device broadcast a series of pings, as opposed to the clang of the Oikomi pipes. Jack says he wanted Humphrey to know precisely where he and Canevero were.

When we were ready, I sent Barry to take a position to the right of the whale. One of the reasons I picked Barry for the job was that I knew I could trust him to do what I said. I also knew he knew as much about what we were doing as I did, which wasn't a hell of a lot. Anyway, when he got between the whale and the west levee, on the side where the press was standing, I proceeded to move carefully to the left of the animal, and I mean carefully. I didn't want to spook him. I will never forget that pectoral slap.

We were right in the middle of the slough, and about fifty to sixty feet from the bridge. Humphrey was calm, which was wonderful. Barry and I were about seventy feet apart at this point, so the whale had room to swim in a circle between us, which he did, around and around. I let him go on for a while, to get used to us on his flanks, and then I started moving my boat backward and forward, at an angle, to move the whale toward Barry and close the space. I closed it eventually to a distance of about fifteen to twenty yards.

It was like I could almost touch Barry, and I know I could have touched the whale. My wheel is on the right side of the boat, and the animal's hump came almost up to the window. The whole thing was like a sandwich. I was on one side, Barry the other, and the whale was the meat. He drifted back and forth. He would move over to Barry and nudge his boat, and he came back and did the same thing to mine. It seemed to me we were all friends again. Everything was peaceful; I think he knew we were on his side.

It may not have looked that way at other parts of the slough, however, because when the whale started to nudge me, I got a call from John Carroll on the Coast Guard vessel.

"Whale One," he said, "this is Zero Seven."

"This is Whale One," I replied. "Go."

"Do you realize the whale is right underneath you?"

I felt like saying, "No kidding," but I said, "Roger that." Then when I looked over, the whale sank a little bit. It moved toward Barry, but it didn't seem like it was doing so on purpose. I don't know for sure, but it looked to me like it was tired and just drifting. I think it may have gone to sleep. Whatever it was doing, it began to float at an angle between our boats, the head toward me and the tail towards Barry.

We maneuvered to straighten it up. We wanted to get it pointed directly at the bridge, which was only thirty feet away at this time. We also wanted to get it between the tenth and eleventh pilings, where the opening was best. When we did that, it was still lazy, still listless, maybe even still asleep. I yelled out the window to Barry to goose the engines. I wanted to give Humphrey a little boost, to remind it why the hell we were there, and that did it. Humphrey went straight forward then, right at the goddamned bridge.

The next thing anyone knew was that the whale began slapping the water again, this time from inside the pilings. It swam in, twisted around, rolled on its side, and pounded the surface like it was stuck. "Oh, damn," Jack said. Peigin Barrett turned away in horror. Barry Canevero watched in angry silence. Then the bridge started to shake, from one end to the other, vibrating like a clothesline in a storm. Jack thought the structure would collapse. The animal was beating it like a rug. He told everyone, by radio, to stand clear.

Several operation officers were standing on the bridge. Worse, it was also crowded with scores of young people from the California Conservation Corps. John Passerello had put the kids in place to drop that plastic curtain over the side, if Humphrey got through. Jack didn't know they were there. They were lying down so they would not scare the whale. Everyone agrees that if the bridge had fallen, the whale, some officials, and a good lot of youngsters might have died.

The bridge shook for a few minutes, until the whale stopped struggling and disappeared. There was one long moment of uncertainty, as the water became still. Then Barry Canevero took the radio to say there was a footprint on the other side of the span. News reporters raced to see. Peigin Barrett grabbed Diana Reiss in a hug, and bedlam broke.

Humphrey was free.

Jake Jacoby noticed it was 4:01 on that Friday afternoon. Everyone cheered and Saint Jude was in her heaven. The CCC stood up to shout hosannas and were finally able to drop the plastic barrier. Mark Ferrari shook hands all around. A Coast Guard member said he wished the marine service still served grog. Jaded members of the press crew also applauded.

Jake says the whale "started to boogie" after that. He was quite obviously as happy about his escape as were those who engineered the breakout. Jack says the whale was now moving at three to four knots toward the Sacramento River, toward more salt and more space, and the rescue boats followed like whistle-blowing floats in a parade of celebration.

Even the federal government got in on the emotion. Sheridan Stone of NMFiS was backslapping with the best of them. Jack says he mentioned to Stone on the way down to the water that he had inadvertently lost one of the government sounding devices, the four-thousand-dollar machines that ping, but the fisheries official was "so elated that he didn't seem to care."

The merrymaking continued for some time, as the whale continued downwater. Eventually Jack had to put on the lid. He reminded the boat crews that they still had a job to do, and he was quite right. Humphrey swam into the Sacramento River that evening, and then down to Rio Vista, where he stopped again when he was confronted by yet another bridge.

chapter eight

HUMPHREY THE WHALE HAD A TEFLON NATURE. HE WAS nothing if not slippery. The rescue teams could keep attendance during the day, but when eventide descended and deliverance was called on account of the dark, the cetacean wandered on his own, hither and yon, mostly yon. When he was pushed from Shag Slough on October 25, he was left for the night near Rio Vista, but when dawn broke the following morning, great balls of fire, he was back in Shag Slough. He hadn't yet gone under the bridge at Liberty Island, but there he was, the big dummy, traveling precariously northward again, troubling trouble, flirting with deja vu, and courting catastrophe.

The Coast Guard was still in port shining boots for the day. Jack Findleton and the others were at the table with their eggs. Humphrey might plainly have blundered into the quagmire again were it not for a chance intercession. Someone happened to see the whale on its way and reported the occasion to a Liberty Island ranch foreman named Stanley Gale. He in turn notified his superiors, who told him to send one of the employees to the water to stop the animal. Say what? The federal government and the state of California had not, so far, stopped the animal, but thirty-four-year-old Mike Covello rubbed the sleep from his eyes and complied.

Covello is a mechanic at the ranch. He is also evidence that even the smallest hair casts a shadow on the head of human events. He drove along the levee road and encountered the whale about midway up the slough. He says he saw it blowing steam: "It was just off the edge of the bank. When I stopped and got out, I think it looked right at me. I'll never forget it. I live on a farm. A cow is a big thing, but this creature was the size of a cloud. I yelled at it at first. It was only fifty or sixty feet away, but it didn't pay no mind. I thought about throwing stones, but he wouldn't have felt it. He just kept moving, in a zigzag, toward the bridge."

Covello is a small, thin man, curly-haired. He lives with his wife and three children in a house rented from the ranch. He says that on the whole he would rather shoot animals than rescue them. He has a closet full of gaming gear, and no use for the antigun arguments. He hunts animals like soldiers hunt people, by the by; he wears the camouflaged clothing that has been popular with the military since Vietnam, and colors his face with olive drab cosmetics. Older sportsmen say the decoration is bunkum. Most animals can't see colors, but, in this respect, Covello is a fellow of his time. Aftershave and eyeshadow: where are you now, Boy George?

Covello says he wound up chasing Humphrey with a field expedient form of the Oikomi method. He had seen people in the rescue boats banging pipes the day before, so he improvised with a tire iron and a cheater bar. He ran in front of the whale and made as much noise as possible with the instruments, and "damned if it didn't do the job." The whale turned around on a dime, even if reluctantly, and swam south. Covello says he followed by foot at times, and at other times in his truck, banging away, hollering like beJesus. The cetacean set a convoluted course, but Covello kept him moving, and so doing may have single-handedly saved the animal's life.

The last guess can be argued. Humphrey may never have gotten to the bridge that morning or may not have ventured through if he had. The plastic curtain was still ready on the bridge, and a posse of hands had been sent to drop it over the rail if the whale got close. Covello at least prevented the small crisis from becoming another emergency. There's little doubt the whale could have survived another stint in the trap—little doubt except in Covello's mind, that is. He doesn't think he did very much, and newspaper accounts of the episode agree. The stories said Covello's boss chased Humphrey from the slough.

Why did the whale go back up the small creek in the first place? Some biologists revived the theory that Humphrey had a death wish, that he was determined to get to the grave. Others, however, thought it was more likely that he found a small feeding ground in Shag Slough. Whales are like industrial-strength vacuum cleaners in the water; they commonly suck in barrels of food each day. Humphrey had been seen at his plate several times in the slough.

Humpbacks normally live on zooplankton and crustaceans, like shrimp. Science believes the species has rudimentary taste buds, and the whales feed in a variety of ways. They have been observed circling their prey to set up engulfing nets made of bubbles or they may get under their food and trap it against the surface of the water. In either event, the whales swim through the mass with mouths open, and they take in copious amounts of water as well as the smaller matter.

Then there is one more function. When the humpbacks close their mouths, they press their tongues against their palates, forcing everything to sift back through their baleen. The baleen is constructed of material much like human fingernails. It resembles a very wide fork with teeth, and each tooth contains bristles or fibers. When the water is expelled, the food is trapped on the bristles. Each week a great whale may pick fifteen thousand pounds of vittles from its teeth.

Jack and the whale boats got started late again that A.M. There is a bureaucracy even for saving lives, such as safety checks and equipment counts. Besides, it was Saturday:

That meant everyone in the universe was off work, and most of them came to the river to help in the rescue. We had a lot of new people and new boats. We also got an eighty-two-foot Coast Guard cutter, the Point Hyer. *Finally, we had something bigger than Humphrey. The* Point Hyer *had presence! This was the major leagues now; everybody was going all out to assist the whale.*

We got to the water about nine o'clock. By that time, Humphrey was out of Shag Slough, and was swimming around near the intersection of Cache Slough and Steamboat Slough, a mile from the Sacramento River. There is a ferry crossing there. That's where we picked the whale up. We got around it with a line of boats, and then the federal government wanted to try something. Jim Lecky of NMFiS said he was going to attach a radio transmitter to the whale's skin. He said the transmitter would send out signals that would help us keep track of Humphrey after dark.

I wondered about messing around with something like that. I thought it was more important to get on with the rescue and get the whale back to sea, but Lecky was in charge. He did what he wanted. He had gotten a bunch of bamboo poles from Sally Downs in Rio Vista, and he had fixed them with suction-cup transmitters. He said the idea was to drive up to the whale, reach out with the long poles, and attach one or more transmitters to the hide. I didn't have much hope for it, frankly; turned out I was right.

Lecky got into a small Coast Guard boat with his assistant, Sheridan Stone, and it didn't look like they were too comfortable with the assignment. Lecky is a Sphinx; he doesn't show much emotion, but Sheridan was nervous. They made some passes before they got close enough. Then they started poking the animal with the poles. I guess they got one or two stuck on the whale, but, as I say, there wasn't much hope. When Humphrey got moving again, the suction cups fell off, and neither Lecky nor Sheridan talked much about it after that.

The NMFiS officers did not give up, however. They were convinced that affixing radio transmitters would be a valuable scientific contribution. They had visions of tracking Humphrey far out into the ocean, by satellite no less, so they would eventually try three more times to attach signal gadgets, once with a crossbow and arrow. That seemed to contradict the NMFiS rule against touching the whale, or using it for laboratory purposes; on the other hand, a transmitter, had it been successful, might have been a federal score.

It may even have justified the cost of the rescue.

The *Point Hyer* wasn't the only big ship to join the rescue operation at Rio Vista. The U.S. Army has a heavy boat reserve unit in the river port, and it contributed a pair of 115-foot LCUs. The reserve unit is designated as the 481st Transportation Company, and LCU stands for Landing Craft Utility. The boats resemble 225-ton bathtubs, and they are grownup versions of the vessels that dropped Marines and other soldiers on the beaches of World War II. Today, the ships are, for the most part, used to carry cargo. Lieutenant Gregg Smith says that prior to the Humphrey mission, the LCUs had been hauling M-60 tanks from one point in the delta to another.

Lieutenant Smith is second in command at the 481st. He is regular Army, and was in charge of the unit's part in the whale flotilla. He is blonde, six-foot six inches tall, and was twenty-six years old at the time of the rescue.

Lieutenant Smith says John Garamendi asked him to join the operation. He got permission from the Sixth Army Command, Presidio, San Francisco. He says he was initially leery about committing his boats to the rescue. They have half-inch plating and can survive torpedo blasts, but there were other safety concerns. The lieutenant did not want to bump into Jack Findleton, or, saints preserve us, the whale! The LCUs would survive either collision, certainly, but Gregg Smith would never be chief of staff. Still, it was time for a weekend drill, and chasing a whale was better than hauling tanks.

Not incidentally, chasing the whale would also give Lieutenant Smith and his men the chance to perform before what may have been the largest audience ever gathered on the banks of the Sacramento River. The Saturday crowd at Rio Vista alone was estimated to be between eight thousand and ten thousand. People flew up from Los Angeles. Locals put out beach umbrellas. Lawrence Hersey from Nevada said he normally spends weekends in Las Vegas; gambling is his revolt against boredom, but he drove to the delta instead, where he fascinated a date by playing blackjack on his car hood and giving odds on the whale's prospects at Rio Vista Bridge. "Two to one," he said.

The crowds were so large by noon that police began to worry about safety of another kind. One motorist, for instance, was so busy looking for the whale that he drove his car off the levee road and almost into the river. Another driver was so absorbed that he collided with the vehicle in front of him on the bridge. Then there was the T-shirt salesman who failed to keep an eye on his table when the activity in the water picked up; he lost twenty-five garments to a person or persons unknown, as the police say it, and he said the thieves probably set up a table of their own.

Jody Vickery of Rio Vista said the crowds disturbed the community peace, and she was "disgusted." John Bulik told reporters that he wished everyone would go back home. P.J. Ojeda, who runs a windsurfing business, said he lost the entire weekend to the whale. At least one man who lives on the river says he had to protect his property with a weapon: "Most of the people, they were okay, but some were tubs of guts. There were two guys in a van who couldn't find a parking place, so they tried to abandon their heap in my driveway. I greeted them with a two by four. It was the biggest thing I had."

Oh, tribulation. Every town should have that kind of invasion. When Mayor Terry Curtola of Vallejo heard of it, he told a newsman: "We have spent three and a half years trying to get a new marine attraction in our community [an aquarium]. All the people in Rio Vista had to do was sit there."

It was a long morning for Jack and the boat crews. First, the fisheries people insisted on trying to plug the whale with that transmitter, wasting time. Then they delivered a second blow to the schedule.

There we were. We had coaxed the whale down to the bridge. We were ready to push him through. There were thousands of people watching from the shore, and the next thing that happened was that someone from the Coast Guard came over to my boat and gave me something wrapped in a piece of blue plastic. When I took it, I knew immediately what it was; it was an automatic shotgun.

I thought, hey, what's going on? I mean, nobody told me anything about a gun. I am the captain of my boat. I am in charge of what comes and goes, and here they are giving me a gun. I hate guns. I've hated guns ever since Vietnam. I had to kill people with guns. I saw my first sergeant blow his leg off with a gun. I don't even like to be around guns. What was the purpose of it anyway? We were trying to save the whale, not shoot it. Like they say, one atom bomb can ruin your whole day.

Besides, there were boats all around, and there were all these people watching. I couldn't imagine that anyone was going to shoot a weapon under the circumstances. If someone were, I didn't like the idea of being part of it. Most of the folks on the operation would be going home after it was over, but the river is my home. This is where I work. I didn't want people to think I had anything to do with firing shots on the water, a few hundred feet from the edge of a town.

So I put the gun in my cabin and secured it. When Sheridan Stone got back aboard, I asked him what was happening. He said NMFiS had decided to shoot cracker shells to motivate the whale. I didn't know what cracker shells were. Neither did anyone else on my boat. Sheridan said the shells were harmless; all they did was make a loud noise. I had to make a decision based on that. I said, all right, if NMFiS insisted on firing the damn things, they had to do it as safely as possible, in the air, and away from boats and people.

That didn't satisfy Debbie Ferrari, however. She was hysterical. I remember I gave the gun to Sheridan. He sat there with it cradled on his knees, and she just tore into him. That scared me, too. In terms of having a gun on board, I told Debbie this is not the time or place to get into a heated debate. When she would not stop badgering Sheridan, I had to get physical. I picked her up from the stern of the boat and deposited her in a seat in the cabin.

Then I became the villain too. I was suddenly Joe Federal. I had supposedly given up my commitment to help the whale. She said she wanted off the boat. When I asked her to calm down, she said she was being kidnapped and held against her will. I told her to calm down. Her husband, Mark, even told her to cool it. It was a hell of a tussle. I had raised my voice before, but I hadn't touched anyone. It was very bad.

Jack says Stone never loaded his gun. Diana Reiss says he always looked "scared to death during the operation," and this time more than ever. NMFiS agents on another boat fired two shots, however, without warning anyone on the river. Debbie said she was quitting the operation. Mark Ferrari demanded an autopsy if anything happened to the whale. Peigin Barrett was watching from the bridge at the time. She says she was outraged: "A few people had been told about the cracker bombs, but most of us had no idea what was taking place. What if the whale had been spooked? What if it had charged a boat? The shooting would be indefensible."

The whale operation almost broke in pieces when the shells were fired. A meeting on shore was hastily convened to try to salvage the greater purpose. Jim Lecky of NMFiS presided, humbled and confessional, burdened with crosses and losses, smiling awkwardly as if he had just been caught picking flowers in the park. Barrett complained. The Ferraris said the shots were spurious. Jack spoke for the boat crews: "I am not comfortable with this kind of thing. If this kind of thing is going to continue, I am going to pull out of the operation."

Lecky said the cracker shells that were spent did not contain any shot. He said they were used to make noise, period. The shells contained paper firecrackers that disintegrated when they exploded, just like the backyard variety on the Fourth of July. Lecky said the shots were to be used to prod the beast through the bridge, so he'd have a better chance for survival.

As for the shock to the crews and volunteers, Lecky apologized. He said he did not announce the plan, because he did not want anyone to protest it. Thomas Jefferson, answer your phone. Lecky suggested that he had hoped the shots would be successful, and then any grumblings would be lost in the cheers. He did not admit error, fat chance, but he promised that the guns and shells would be put away. Jack withdrew his threat to quit. Ditto for Debbie. The wounded operation was healed.

Errors that are quickly put behind are usually the least damaging. This time the mistake lingered on. Thirty minutes after the cracker shells were fired, Humphrey slid across a shoal on the east side of the river, and became wedged in the muck. It was the third time the great beast had been stranded on land in sixteen days; most whales never do it at all.

One volunteer said the whale may have been scared by a wandering Coast Guard boat, rather than by the shells, but Dr. Ken Norris raised the possibility that the explosion could have made the animal temporarily deaf and disoriented. Debbie and Mark Ferrari were convinced that the shots were to blame, and held Lecky and Stone fully responsible.

Every camera and pair of binoculars turned toward the beached animal. Traffic stopped completely on the Rio Vista Bridge. Jim Lecky confided to a friend that he had visions of the whale rotting in the sand, while he tried to explain to the nation what he had done. Joyce Everett also looked on; she is the bakery owner, and president of the Humphrey Fan Club:

"It just gave me goose pimples to see it so much out of the water. I wanted to cheer when it started to work its way free. Its big tail moved, its flippers caught hold, and you could see the ripples in its skin as it moved. That was one of the most tremendous things I've ever experienced. I was out of breath, when Humphrey was swimming again."

Humphrey did not seem the worse for wear. He took some initial spins around the shoal vicinity, and when the rescue operation resumed, he was nosy as ever. One of the onlookers, Donald Phipps, says the animal inspected some of the larger craft, buzzed by the bridge, and almost tipped over a small boat: "It was a skiff, like a dinghy. Humphrey went right beside it. I don't know how he missed it with his tail. I looked at the guy in the boat. I swear he must have had to change his pants."

Events finally got underway in earnest at mid-afternoon, and Jack could not have been more pleased. The charter-boat captain wanted to believe that government, in its fashion, was sorry for the shooting incident. It certainly bent to the will of the majority this time. Jack says it was the first time since Vietnam that he personally saw federal officials admit that collaboration comes before command in the dictionary. Jim Lecky, with a Mona Lisa smile, was still an enigma, but Sheridan Stone seemed contrite, and Jack grew rather fond of him.

What's more, Jack didn't think the whale beaching was necessarily the government's fault. NMFiS shot the cracker shells, but that may only have been a contributing factor. Humphrey seemed in the main to be up to its old antics; when it was bothered by boats, and pestered by pressures, it inevitably responded with a threatening signal that was rewarded with peace and serenity, the ole devil. It played various parts in the drama that it wrote. Sometimes it was the susceptible alien, sometimes the oversensitive giant, and sometimes it was naught but an old trouper, addressing the audience for laughs.

Jack says he told the boat crews that they would have to push the whale under the Rio Vista Bridge the same way they had pushed it under the Liberty Island Bridge, with a pinching action:

I said all of the boats would join in driving the whale close to the span, and Barry Canevero and I would force the final few feet. We didn't think there would be any serious problem. Humphrey should have been getting used to obstacles by then, and the police had closed the bridge to traffic to eliminate noise. The police also asked people who were working on the bridge, painters I think, to stop what they were doing.

Then a funny thing happened. Humphrey started to ham it up. I mean it. The whale was enjoying its time in the spotlight. We came up behind it on one side of the river, and it would turn and hurry to the other. Then we would go over to where it was. Humphrey would then reverse itself and shoot back to the original side. The people on the shore loved it. They cheered Humphrey's every move. When it came under my boat to give me the slip, they cheered even louder—thousands of people, all roaring.

The thing that sticks in my mind is that the people on shore turned the whole business into a big contest. It was Man versus Beast, and they clapped when the beast got its licks. When Humphrey got away from us the first time, the score was Whale One, Boats Zero. When it slipped away again, the score was Whale Two, Boats Zero. I know I can't say that Humphrey was invigorated by all this, but it seemed to be. It was part of a big show we were putting on, free of admission, and it was making the most of the spotlight.

The bridge was closed for ninety minutes. Traffic was backed up for miles on either side of the river. Bridge-tender Dale Gearing says he stayed in the tower, by the radio for emergencies, otherwise he joined everyone else in the whale watch. He also raised the long lift in the middle of the bridge to a height of 140 feet; that is normally the way large ships pass under the structure, and the authorities thought that Humphrey might want to negotiate the same route.

Gearing says the stranded traffic was orderly. Some people got out of their cars to get refreshments for the wait. One fellow left his date in the car, just before the bridge reopened, and she was forced to drive across herself. That led to a problem, of course. She didn't know where her boyfriend had gone to get food. She stopped in a half dozen eateries, explaining the predicament, and asking each customer: "Have you seen my boyfriend? He is a real jerk."

Actually, the guy probably went to Granny's. That's a fast food stand in Rio Vista, very close to the bridge. The owner, B.J. Simon, is a mellow gentleman, who has blue veins on his red face and has a World War II haircut. He says he bought the stand twenty years ago. "It was called Franny's then. I wanted to change the name, so I asked a painter how much it would cost. He said he'd do the whole thing for sixty-five dollars or change one letter for ten. I changed F to G. Best deal I ever made."

Granny's is a relic of another age. It is shaped like the boxcar diners that were beau monde in the 1940s. The hamburgers are fresh, not frozen. The french fries are cut in different lengths, if you can imagine, and the clerk doesn't wear a cap. It's not all rustic remembrance, however. Simon maintains a sit-down wing, where the tables are covered with the same kind of easy-cleaning, forever-shining Formica that is found at, say, Wendy's.

Simon uses one of the tables for his office. He is surrounded by diners who have long ashes on their cigarettes. Simon chews tobacco himself, or sucks it, or rolls it around, whatever. No one minds. It will rain soon. Simon says Granny's was full to busting when Humphrey was in the river. "I had two cooks and four girls workin.' We still closed right sharp at 8:00 P.M., though. I never got in this business to make a killin'."

That girl who lost a boyfriend wasn't alone. One lady almost lost a husband when the whale came through. The woman was trying to get across the bridge to attend her own wedding, when she was foiled by stopped traffic. She then went to Sally Downs's bait shop to call ahead on the public phone. Sally says she was all dressed up, pretty, and bawling.

Then there was Eric Dalquist. He was a substitute tackle on the Rio Vista High School football team, and he was stuck on the east side of the bridge before the homecoming game. He was frenetic. The big night, his girlfriend would be watching, and he wouldn't be there. He used a line of scrimmage option, however, the old quarterback sneak. He hustled a ride across the river with a sympathetic boatsman.

Coach Dick Nunes says he might not have bothered. The Rio Vista Rams were shut out by Justin High School, thirty-two to oops. Nunes says he was happy to know that at least one of his players was on the ball that night, but it's too bad Humphrey didn't knock the bridge down: "Maybe the other team wouldn't have shown up." The coach can be forgiven his annoyance; the Rams didn't win a game all season.

Well, wait until next year. Jack says Humphrey was the home team anyway on October 26.

I can't get over the idea that the rescue was a sport at the bridge. It was Us against the Whale, and I'm convinced he knew it. On two occasions, he went under the bridge on the east side, then swam along the bridge to the west side, and came back under again. Each time he did it, the crowd would applaud. It was so obvious. I think Humphrey swam under the one side, and then said, "Wow, that was a kick. I think I'll go back over and see Jack again."

I had to laugh a little. By the same token, I was irritated. I didn't want to play around all day, so Barry and I decided the fun was over. I brought all the boats up tight, to trap the animal against the east end of the bridge. There was plenty of water there, and he seemed to like to go under at that spot. Barry got on one side and I got on the other. We just inched him in the right direction, and followed him through the bridge supports. I think it was about 4:30 in the afternoon. I got the radio and told everyone to catch up.

I can still hear the noise. Finally the crowd was cheering the whale boats as well as the whale. I had begun to get worried that the people on the banks had been angered by the firing of the cracker shells, and blamed the rescue teams, but I guess that wasn't the case. They hollered, and Humphrey continued down the river on the eastern side. Highway 161 runs along the dyke on the east side, and I could see the folks getting into their cars to follow us down. It was quite a pageant. Boats in the water and automobiles on the road.

Humphrey was moving at a good pace now. We kept in formation on his rear, and banged the Oikomi pipes. The only trouble was that the sun would be going down soon, and we couldn't push him at night. I started thinking about a good place to park the whale. John Carroll of the Coast Guard was on my boat, and we both thought of Decker Island. That's where the animal beached himself on the way upriver. We thought we could maneuver Humphrey into Horseshoe

Bend, behind the island, and then block him in there for the rest of the night.

Unfortunately, it got dark before we reached the island. The only light we had was from the moon and the boat lamps. We turned him toward Horseshoe Bend, but he slipped away and swam toward the island's middle shore. There were some fishermen in a rowboat at that location. They didn't have any lights on the thing, and they were in twenty to thirty feet of water. Lieutenant Carroll grabbed the microphone, and he was very urgent. He said, "There is a whale directly underneath your boat. Go immediately to the shore and stay there."

Dick Whiteside, one of my whale boat skippers, also had a close encounter with Humphrey that night. He said the animal surfaced right alongside his vessel in the dark. Otherwise, we simply lost sight of it. We tried to herd him to the north end of Decker Island, and into the mouth of Horseshoe Bend, but I don't know if we did or not. We turned off our motors and heard him splash; that's all I can say. When we left for home, we didn't know what he'd do next.

John Carroll sent a SITREP, gad, to COMCOGARDGRU, double gad, San Francisco. He said the cutter *Point Hyer* had "commenced a blockade" of the area around Decker Island to prevent water traffic from disturbing the whale. There wasn't much worry of abuse, however, except accidentally. The only citation the Coast Guard issued during the Humphrey visit was to a commercial boat, whose captain refused to give way.

Most of the rescue people stayed in Rio Vista again. They bunked in the Army reserve barracks, at the Coast Guard station, and in spare rooms provided in local homes. Some of the volunteers also dozed at taverns in the town, where one heard the following: "I was painting my boat, when a can of varnish fell overboard and a fish swallowed it. Yes, it died a horrible death, but it had a lovely finish."

Todd Hause was the only member of the operation who stayed on duty that night. He was from the California Marine Mammal Center, and he camped in a boat, on the down side of the bridge, to bang on pipes and make other noises until the sun came up. He said he was worried that Humphrey, despite his ordeal, might decide to turn around and come back upriver again. As it happened, volunteer Hause was on the money.

chapter nine

BENJAMIN DISRAELI USED TO COMPLAIN THAT, WHILE THE anticipated seldom occurs, the least expected generally happens. He must have known about rescuing whales. Just when events began to look most promising on the Humphrey operation, just when the bridges were behind and the ocean was ahead, the impetuous Mysticeti set the mission on its ear by setting a new course. Here was an animal who had found his way from cold oceans to warm seas over years of global migration. Here was a beast who could swim from Sitka to the Baja, with only the compass of the mind; yet here was a silly twit who, in the wading waters of the Sacramento River Delta, could not, to the anguish of millions, distinguish north from south.

Jack Findleton and the boat crews spent one more day after the labors at the Rio Vista bridge, prodding Humphrey all the way to Pittsburg, which is just before the Carquinez Strait. The strait leads into San Pablo Bay, which, at last, connects with the San Francisco estuary and the Pacific Ocean. When the operation stopped for the night after that drive, the whale was only forty miles from home, and all it had to do was pay attention. It didn't. It turned around in the dark and swam fourteen miles upriver to Decker Island, where it had beached two weeks earlier, and where it was once again flirting with the dicey enigmas of the upper delta.

The rescue leaders were not pleased. The whale was not just difficult, it was eccentric, and the operation had become circular. Jim Lecky told news reporters, who were also beginning to droop, that something like this could continue indefinitely. The operation could control the whale to a degree during the day, but Humphrey was on its own to blunder about at night. Lecky suggested that it had gotten to be a case of one step forward, one step back, and meanwhile expenses were piling up. Some team members argued that the government still had an obligation to save the endangered mammal, forget the setbacks, but Lecky made up his mind:

"We are suspending this immediate operation."

The statement contained some qualification. Lecky did not say the rescue was terminated permanently, but there were suspicions that might be the intent. Lecky had never considered Humphrey to be the primary item on the agenda of the National Marine Fisheries Service, and there were pressures to get on to other duties. Besides, the rescue teams had been splintered by the arrival of a new work week. Saturday and Sunday volunteers had returned to their jobs. Dutra Construction called in its boats. The Army reservists went home. Jack says he only had two rescue vessels, *Sportfish I* and *Fishing Fool III,* in the water when the mission was canceled.

Incidentally, Jack was as disappointed as anyone when the rescue stopped, and again, there is a Vietnam analogy. "I thought, here it goes again. The only difference was that there were no jungles. We win the battles, but we lose the war."

Peigin Barrett says she sent her volunteers home with sorrow, which was a companion to pique. She remained stationed herself, as did a few other members of the marine mammal center, but there was hell to pay just the same. "We've had hundreds of complaints at the center; some of them from our own members. Everyone wants to know how we could just turn our backs on the whale. I wonder the same thing myself."

Shoes must fall in pairs, when circumstances falter, and the second one was dropped by the state of California. John and Beverly Passerello, of the Office of Emergency Services, told the press they had come across a new and possibly perturbing theory concerning the cetacean. They said they had gone home to rest, when the operation was put on hold, and had read books on whales. They said they learned that the birthing season for humpbacks begins in November, which was just around the corner, and that female whales frequently seek out private territory in which to deliver their calves.

In short, Humphrey, or Humphretta, might be pregnant.

Understand, it was a slow news period, and journalists are alarmists; that's their way of attracting a crowd. NMFiS representatives said the Passerello idea had no credence. Debbie Ferrari protected her original calculation that the humpback was a hunk. Still, nobody could speak conclusively one way or the other. The whale had never shown its ventral (under) side. The animal was so fat it might conceal a pregnancy anyway, and Ferrari admitted there was a twenty percent chance that the mammal *could* be female; hence the story was a front page bulletin: "Humphrey May Have Bread in the Oven."

That possibility generated a set of complications that had not been theretofore considered, and it caused a reconsideration of everything that had taken place for the past two and a half weeks. The rescue operation was nourished with the conviction that the whale was either lost or sick, and, in either eventuality, needed assistance. Now there was reason to doubt and even to abhor that thinking. If Humphrey was pregnant, and merely looked for seclusion, the rescue effort had been an inexcusable intrusion, not to say harassment; the biologists had blundered intolerably; the volunteers had invaded a maternity ward; Captain Jack was pushing a mother around.

Most importantly, the story revived the issue of government involvement in the natural world. Some volunteers wondered if that wasn't the premeditated purpose of the flap. The state had not been enthusiastic about involvement with Humphrey, and even when it joined the operation, it played a subordinate role. Maybe the Passerellos had released the pregnancy scoop for ulterior motives, maybe to get California to the egress. There's no proof, and state officers say the speculation is absurd, but Senator John Garamendi notes that the Passerellos drifted away from the operation after the headlines, and the California assistance essentially ended.

The headlines had a short run. They could not be supported by corroborating evidence. The humpback had seemed plump when it was beached at various times, but that may have been from fortunate feedings. The whale did not show any other signs of being in a family way. Ron Reuther of the Whale Center in Oakland pointed out that whales have been dropping their calves in the open seas ever since man started keeping account. Debbie Ferrari added one more time that Humphrey had scar markings on his back that were probably etched in combat, and they are a primary means of identifying males.

Humphretta indeed. There were some jokes about the affair that we won't mention. Oh well, one: Humphrey had a date with one of those well-armored sturgeons. They had a nice time until they began to watch the moon rise over MaKenson. "Tell me," Humphrey asked, "are you the opposite sex or am I?"

The story of the imagined pregnancy illustrated one of the scholastic oddities of the Humphrey experience. There was a dearth of truly expert opinion at the scene. Dr. Ken Norris of UCSC had genuine credentials. The Ferraris had experience, if no doctorates. Jim Lecky, Sheridan Stone, Diana Reiss, and a few more were researchers: otherwise, the experts at the operation were often created by media pronouncement.

Dr. Hal Markowitz is a biologist at San Francisco State University who did not participate in the rescue. He says he followed the news, however, and was amused to see so many of his students being interviewed as "scientists." They would come to class afterwards, he says, and slink into their chairs amid the hoots and sniggers of classmates: "I know you think I thought I knew what I meant, but I don't know if I did."

Jim Dixon of the California Fish and Game Department continued to assist what was left of the rescue operation, and so did his wife, Kristin. She was hired by NMFiS to study the tides and currents in the delta to see whether they had an effect on the habits of the whale. She is a mathematics graduate of Purdue University, and she says she wanted to find out specifically whether Humphrey utilized movements of the water.

It did. Dixon says she tracked the whale through eleven sequences of changing tides and currents, and discovered that it moved against the currents in nine of them. That makes sense, of course. Every fisherman knows that sea creatures ebb and flow with the tides, but NMFiS officials say they did not have data regarding whales, so it may be one of the few things of lasting value learned about Humphrey.

That information may prove to be of more than just scientific interest. The information might be useful if ever a whale comes off the ocean again. Dixon says Humphrey probably came through the Golden Gate during an extreme ebb tide, swimming against the flow, so that might be the time to watch during migrations. Then, if a whale does come inland, it may be possible to drive it immediately back out when the current makes a change.

The federal government continued to monitor the whale in the water. NMFiS also continued the attempts to decorate it with a radio transmitter. Jack says the government did not want to go on losing contact with the animal every night. There could be no more progress if it just wandered where it wanted after dark, so the agency hired an oceanographer from Oregon State University to stick Humphrey electronically:

"That was Dr. Bruce Mate. He was a dedicated man, and he thought big. When Jim Lecky had tried to tag the whale at Rio Vista Bridge, he was using suction cups and a simple device that let out a small signal. Dr. Mate wanted to pin a high-technology transmitter in Humphrey's hump, which could be picked up by a satellite. He had done it before, he said, and had been able to track whales out into the ocean."

Jack says the oceanographer had troubles in the delta, however. High winds and rough waters disrupted his efforts. Sheridan Stone took longitude and latitude readings, so the satellite connection could be synchronized, and Dr. Mate tried repeatedly, but unsuccessfully, to drive the tags home with a long stick. Eventually, after four days' effort, NMFiS was able to pin a pair of transmitters on the beast, one at the dorsal fin, the other higher on the back.

The transmitters were secured with small harpoon hooks, and it was the first time Humphrey had been intentionally penetrated. Fisheries officials had said earlier that the whale should not be violated in any way, but they were determined to fix the transmitters. They said the hooks were treated with antibiotics, and Dr. Mate agreed that the huge animal could not feel the bite through his foot-thick blubber.

The transmitters were three inches wide, and they had eighteen-inch antennas. It's unclear whether they worked at all. Some officials say there were early readings; others doubt signals were recorded at any time. It may be that the transmitters were too low on the body to send beeps; water acts as a barrier. More than likely, the tags were not embedded securely, and, after all the kibitzing, fell off as Humphrey rolled around.

The transmitter failure was expensive. By one reckoning, at least two thousand dollars was spent on time, people, and equipment; but the federal government had become accustomed to large numbers in the Humphrey saga. The whale operation had ceased to be a purely voluntary and humanitarian action. When all of the bills were paid some months later, the total expenditure was ninety thousand dollars. National Marine Fisheries paid sixty thousand of that, and the rest was covered by public donations.

It was a whale of a sum, and it was probably due to the federal presence. Many of the people who worked for nothing at the start of the Humphrey visit asked for payment contracts when NMFiS became fully involved. Mark and Debbie Ferrari were volunteers for the California Marine Mammal Center at first, and later charged expenses to the government. Bernie Krause, Diana Reiss, and most of the other specialists were also compensated for costs, and, in Krause's case, time too.

Dutra Construction was given many thousands of dollars for the use of their boats, employees, and equipment. Jack Findleton and Barry Canevero were paid for their time as well. The government even took care of some of the extraordinary expenses incurred by the military forces on hand. The state was reimbursed for part of its contributions, and there were payments for research work, gasoline, boat rentals, air tickets, motels, and communication installations.

Peigin Barrett of CMMC paid for thirty thousand worth of the latter items. She used money raised by a Sacramento television station and other collections. She says NMFiS was prohibited from taking the donations to pay the bills, so the agency asked CMMC to do it on its own. Barrett says the NMFiS regional director, Charlie Fullerton, told her he was happy that donated money could be used to pay part of the costs, because some of the demands were excessive.

Barrett agrees. She thinks Jack, Barry Canevero, and Bill Dutra could have been more generous. One fellow who may not have participated at all asked for $250 for "wear and tear." She says she paid almost everything, however, and, in fairness, she adds that it probably would have been unreasonable to expect working people to give up everything for the cause. She received her usual salary, for instance.

Barrett was one of the few people from CMMC to be paid,

however. There are only four staff positions at the center, and the rest of the 150 members strictly volunteered, so did dozens of people in Rio Vista and scores of businesses in the delta. Bill Gordon, the director of the National Marine Fisheries, said the ninety thousand dollars outlay should be considered with that in mind; he says if everyone had charged for their time to save Humphrey, the bill would have been $500,000.

By the end of October, then, the whale had become a half-million-dollar property, but he continued to roam the area like a patch-pocketed Bedouin, with no fixed address and no apparent intent. He cruised the docks at Pittsburg, where he produced a brief, but critically acclaimed, comedy. He hung around the Pacific Gas & Electric discharged culvert, where the water was warmer than anywhere else. The Contra Costa Sheriff's Department said he also went up the San Joaquin River for a few hours, where he explored the other distributary that forms the Sacramento River Delta.

The animal was so mobile that authorities could not keep pace, and the public was encouraged to report all sightings. Logs were reported, as were fishermen at dusk, and there were one or two calls from someone named Jonah saying he was sitting in a dark, damp room, surrounded by complaining fish. A newspaper printed one story of a boatsman who called police to say he had seen the whale swimming about one mile southwest of the Pacific Gas and Electric plant. When officials plotted the location on the charts, they determined that Humphrey had coasted directly into downtown Antioch.

This was absurd. Operation Whale Rescue had deteriorated to burlesque. Peigin Barrett says complacency had taken root, fertilized in part by satiation. The state had no further interest, the press returned to writing about AIDS and sewer bonds, and, most seriously, the federal government was preparing to take a powder. Jim Lecky of NMFiS said he wanted to pack up and go home, another way of saying cave in.

Nonetheless, the whale was still in Draconian trouble. No one had expected it to survive this long in fresh water. Barrett says she discussed the matter with Dr. Diana Reiss, and they asked State Senator John Garamendi to apply some sort of resuscitation. They met him in the kitchen of the Coast Guard station at Rio Vista. He said the road to success is always under construction, or something like that, but he had an idea.

The senator asked Barrett and Reiss to arrange a telephone conference with notable marine scientists across the country. He said they might be able to suggest a fresh approach. The teleconference would likewise serve to revive public interest through the media, and that would put new pressure on the federal government commitment. Yogi Berra said the game ain't over until it's over; there was still the ninth inning.

Jack had gone home for a couple of days, and he didn't know if he'd be called back or not. It was nice to have a meal at the table again, and, "What do you know, Kansas City won the World Series." He was not comfortable, however. He remained with the whale emotionally. When he came home from Vietnam, he was never at ease until the war was settled. The same thing happened now: "I read the news and I saw the television roundups. I couldn't wait to get back and get my whale to the ocean."

He returned to the delta the last day of the month. A marine veterinarian had been summoned to make a visual examination of Humphrey, and Jack was asked to provide transportation. The veterinarian was Dr. Laura Gage from an aquarium in Vallejo. Jack says she was businesslike, as medicos tend to be. She made notes on the whale's appearance, and measured the time between its blows. She also watched the animal move in the water, recording speed and animation.

She said the Humphrey looked remarkably healthy, far better than he had in Shag Slough. The creature seemed to be responding to the increased salinity in the lower delta. "He was back on the oats," as Jack concluded. Dr. Gage told reporters that the cetacean was still discolored, as it had been in the slough, indicating the continuation of skin sluffing, but, other than that, "he has a nice, healthy blow, and he seems to be moving very strong in the water."

For his part, Jack concurred. Over the distance, he had come to know the back of the whale like the front of his hand, but there was no time to compare observations: "I told Dr. Gage that we had to get back to the teleconference in Sacramento. One of the volunteers got someone to fly us in an airplane. That's when I began to think there was hope for the operation yet. I don't often get rides in private planes."

The teleconference was held in the Water Resources Bureau in Sacramento. John Garamendi coordinated the calls with Charlie Fullerton, and that in itself was encouraging. Fullerton is the regional director of the National Marine Fisheries Service. He had stayed away from the first part of the Humphrey operation, and sent Jim Lecky in his stead, but now he was assuming the federal command. Garamendi was elated. Fullerton was not a marine mammal expert, by any means, and he has a careless personality when dealing with people, but he was the boss. Lecky had been timid; Fullerton had muscle. His last-minute arrival was an omen.

Aside from the local experts, the following people participated in the conference: Dr. Ken Norris; Dr. Howard Brahem, director of the National Marine Mammal Laboratories in Seattle; Dr. Bill Watkins, Woods Hole Oceanographic Institution, Massachusetts; Dr. Jay Sweeney, a veterinarian with Marineland of the Pacific, San Diego; Dr. Lou Herman, Professor of Marine Behavior, the University of Hawaii; Dr. Frank Aubrey, Hubbs/Sea World Marine Research Institute, Seattle; John Robinson, NOAA, Seattle; Duane Johnson, California Fish and Game. In addition, there were two men on the line from Canada: Dr. Joseph Geraci, University of Guelph, Ontario and Dr. John Lien of the Whale Research Group Memorial University in Newfoundland.

Some of the scientists had been contacted previously. They all had a working understanding of the Humphrey predicament, but wise though they were, they were short on ideas. Dr. Herman of Hawaii made the only concrete proposal. He suggested that an attempt be made to lure the animal to the sea with tape recordings. He said he knew the rescuers had already failed to scare Humphrey with the sounds of killer whales, but he thought the beast might still respond if the recordings were friendly. He said his students had made tapes of humpbacks singing and feeding near Alaska, and they had conducted successful tests with them to attract other whales.

There was some argument. Bernie Krause, the audiologist, said he had already decided that tape recordings were like a signpost with no destination. Some of the scientists had similar doubts, but when the conference ended, it was the only idea on the table. What is more uncertain than an *only* idea? No idea. Charlie Fullerton had the helm, and he said it was worth a try.

He asked if Dr. Herman would furnish the feeding tapes, and the biologist said he would put them on an air shipment that day. Fullerton told Lecky to alert the crews that Operation Whale Rescue was ready to resume.

Check that. The rescue would not resume as Operation Whale Rescue, per se. There would be administrative changes too. The National Oceanographic and Atmospheric Administration was sending in one of its hazardous materials teams. The teams are composed of men and women who are trained to take charge during emergencies such as petroleum spills at sea. For the most part, the team took charge of public relations for the emergency in the Sacramento River Delta.

A seasoned NOAA publicist named Hal Alabaster shouldered Jay Ziegler to the side. He also rejiggered the name of the rescue to the NOAA Whale Rescue Operation. Volunteers complained that it was an odious bid to grab the national spotlight that was turning on again, but NOAA is a step higher than NMFiS on the federal organizational chart, and it had the authority to do what it wished. So do book authors, in some respects; Operation Whale Rescue will continue to suffice in this volume.

Life is a series of shipwrecks and salvages. A few days before the rescue recommenced, Jack Findleton and Barry Canevero were sitting on the bow of a boat in the river, smoking cigarettes, steeped in both commiseration and anticipation. They did not like to be chessmen on a board, pushed and pulled by federal fits and starts, but they promised one another that if they ever did get the whale to the Pacific, they would go through the Golden Gate side by side, winners.

"We had all kinds of mixed emotions," Jack says.

We were hot to go, but the damn operation was on one day, off the next. Who knew? I had canceled two fishing clients to that point, and Barry had canceled three. That's something you don't do in the business, not if you want to stay in the business. We were a little down. We felt mistreated. We sat there looking at the water from the bow. The water was calm. Good weather. Pretty soon the sun would set.

Then, lo and behold, we saw the whale in front of us. Hum-

phrey was head on and coming right at us. He was higher out of the water than I had seen him before. It was the best look we got at his body. He could have wiped us out with a tiny flick. He could have sent us flying over the shore, but we knew he wouldn't. He came twenty or thirty yards from us, and then turned smoothly and gracefully away. The whole thing only lasted a minute or so; then he disappeared.

I know I have said we had a personal relationship with the animal, but this was the proof of the pudding. It was astonishing. Both Barry and I felt he came up at that moment to greet us, and to cheer us up. Don't tell me he didn't appreciate what we were doing. He came by to say thanks. He was stroking us a little. It gave me a tremendous emotional lift. It renewed my faith in what we had been doing. I was on top of the world when the sun descended.

chapter ten

ON SUNDAY, NOVEMBER 2, JACK FINDLETON SUMMONED FIFty small boats and large ships to make one more concerted attempt to move Humphrey the errant whale from the confines of the Sacramento River Delta. It was twenty-four days after the leviathan had been initially sighted in the vermicular estuary, three lengthy weeks in the lives of hundreds of people who had been introduced to one another and themselves by common purpose. Debbie Ferrari, the biologist, said the expenditure of time was little enough to be done for an animal in distress, and the ninety thousand dollars it cost was a "wonderful way to spend money," but that was not the cardinal reason the participants gathered again in the morning mists. The real reason, as Napoleon said, was that "impossible" is not good French.

Jack says the lifesaving flotilla was now as big as the navies of some nations. He had to fight to keep it nominally civilian. When the National Oceanic and Atmospheric Administration took charge of the rescue, it had hoped to make it an exclusively governmental operation, but when it passed the word that volunteers would no longer be needed, the volunteers protested. NOAA worried that the civilians did not have the experience to handle Humphrey. The civilians argued that they had become veterans in the trenches of Shag Slough, and, as writers will complain, where were the critics when the pages were blank? The argument ended when the government conceded that the people who had already saved the whale at least twice were competent to do it a third and final time.

Jack says most of the original boat teams were collected for the last drive—the personal friends, the pipe bangers, the boys from Dutra Construction. He had to enlist a squad of new people as well, and the reason was that the herding was going to take place in wider waters:

> We had gotten by fine with six boats in Shag Slough, because it was only a hundred yards across. We realized at the Rio Vista Bridge that the line was getting thin. Now we were down at Antioch and Pittsburg, where the river is a mile from shore to shore, and we were aiming for the wide open spaces of Suison Bay, San Pablo Bay, and, if God was awake, San Francisco Bay. We needed a whole fleet, so I talked with a marina owner in Sacramento, and I was promised fifteen new boats along with their skippers.
>
> I might mention that I had some trouble getting the boats down from the Sacramento marina. The government almost messed it up. I wanted to get the boats as soon on Sunday morning as possible, and the best way to do that was to have them come straight down the Deep Water Shipping Channel, but there are locks at the channel, and it costs 150 dollars to have them opened. I asked Jim Lecky of NMFiS for permission to spend the money, and he said, 'Well, that is, I don't know.' Imagine. I had twenty-five boats that would not cost the government anything, and he was shuffling his feet over a few bucks to save time and gasoline. I told him that he would just have to rely on my judgment. I pooled some money with other people, we got the locks open, and the boats arrived right on time.

The Navy also arrived without delay. Officials from NOAA had asked the service headquarters at Treasure Island for the help. Hence the Army, Navy, and Coast Guard would now be involved, a full-scale mammalian maneuver. The Navy contributed thirty-nine sailors from something called COMSPECBOATU, which, for those of you who learned the ropes from the earlier instruction on acronyms, means Command Special Boat Units. COMSPECBOATU was directed by LCDR (Lieutenant Commander) Paul Schmella, who brought ten PBRs (river patrol boats) and one CCB (command and control boat), which were authorized by COMCIPACTFT (Commander in Chief of the Pacific Fleet). Schmella said the vessels could be used on one condition, that the Navy would be in command of itself. That was all right with Jack, who does not speak in ALPs (alphabetics).

There was one more new boat in the lineup, a thirty-seven-foot pleasure cruiser named *Bootlegger*. It was commanded by a vacationing businessman named Jim Cook, who, by his own reckoning, did not do anything anyone else wouldn't have done, but he did it well. Cook's boat was chosen to lead Humphrey with the tape-recorded sounds. Dr. Lou Herman had sent the tapes from Hawaii, the audiologist Bernie Krause had prepared them for the specific use, and *Bootlegger* would be the carrier. The boat was chosen because it had a generator that created the electricity necessary to power the recording transducer.

Cook says he was just along to drive, and once or twice to substitute a song by Willie Nelson. He was fifty-seven years old. He lived on his boat in a marina near Rio Vista. He says he took a week off his work to help Humphrey: "I'm an apple broker in San Francisco. I arrange to have apples from Washington State sold to people on the Pacific Rim. I sell about one and a half million boxes a year to people in Malaysia, Singapore, Hong Kong, and so on. That's a whole lot of apples. It's about sixty million pounds, or, if you prefer, about a hundred million apples."

Cook says apples are the most widely cultivated fruit in the world, and the best of the trees are cultivated in the Lake Chelan area of eastern Washington State. There are seventy-five hundred apple varieties in the world cupboard, and some twenty-five hundred alone in the United States: Jonathans, Granny Smiths, Crabs. A Canadian named McIntosh tagged one for himself. Johnny Appleseed is buried in Indiana. The Stamin Winesap of a Virginia November makes a pie for all seasons.

Captain Cook sailed with his wife, Sandy. He also helped Bernie Krause and Diana Reiss install the broadcasting system. He says the tapes were played from a machine not unlike those found in millions of homes, but the transducer was a 160-pound, seventeen hundred dollars, state-of-the-art gem lent by the Navy. As for the sounds themselves, Cook says the noise of feeding humpbacks is an amalgamation of squeaks and bellows. He did not get much out of it personally, but then he doesn't feed on plankton in the ocean. He doesn't feed much on apples, either. "Well, I like them, but you get a little tired of them, you know."

One other digression. Just before the operation got underway, Dr. Bernie Krause told Dr. Diana Reiss that he didn't want to play the tape recordings, and the notion should be terminated.
"What?" she said.
"It's a waste of time," he said.
"What do you mean?"
"They won't work."
"You're kidding."
"I mean it. I think we should forget about it."
Reiss says she almost fell out of the boat, but recovered to tell her colleague that he was not Jehovah. "I said the decision had been made, and it did not make any difference what he thought, the tape recordings would be played."

The flotilla left Rio Vista at about 9:00 A.M., and met Humphrey at the mouth of the San Joaquin River. Jack formed the boats in what the Navy calls a reverse wedge, a V with the point upriver, and waited for the audiologists to signal. Bernie Krause made adjustments in the equipment and Dr. Reiss went out in a rubber boat to test for noise level. She says as soon as the tape was turned on, "Humphrey turned around from where he was swimming, and made a beeline for *Bootlegger*."

The noise level was apparently fine. Reiss hurried to the boat. The water was filled with the sound of dining cetaceans. Humphrey had everything on but a napkin, and the fleet procession began. Krause told Captain Cook to take it easy. Reiss says the whale fell just behind the wake of the boat. Jack says that when he got close he could see Humphrey looking up as if summoning the maitre d'. Lou Herman of the University of Hawaii had saved the day; his tapes worked.

Reiss, who is the expert on animal communications, has an explanation. She says the tapes may have represented a call for dinner. She says humpbacks have a complicated feeding ritual, and they often have to coordinate their efforts to get food. The tapes may very well have been the sounds the creatures use to launch an attack on a school of crustaceans, signals for everyone in a pod to join the maneuver; Humphrey had doubtless heard it countless times, and so he obliged.

The audiologists did not want the whale to become too accustomed to the callings, however. There was the chance he could get wise or bored, so they alternated the tapes with dead space and they used various sound levels. They also told Captain Cook to drive the boat in a meandering fashion, to mimic the humpback's normal swimming habits. The result was that Humphrey had at last been had. He followed the boat as directed, mile after mile, hour after hour.

Jim Cook says it seemed to him that the whale was "playing with *Bootlegger*." The animal would come close, fall back, and then go to one side or the other."I don't know if he thought he was actually running with a group of whales, or whether he thought my boat was a whale, but it was like he was racing me, having a grand old splurge. I could look right down his blowhole, and I know he could look right back at me. I got to know him, I think, and understand a little."

Oh, lord, when Humphrey started moving south, the Coast Guard reported that another Mysticeti was moving north. A gray whale had swum inside the Golden Gate Bridge. Wouldn't you know it. No one had prepared for a two-whale undertaking. Unlike Humphrey, however, the second creature took one look at Haight Ashbury, and fortunately beat it back to the migration.

Speaking of ill-portending interruptions, there were clouds accumulating over the Army and Navy vessels in the armada. The two commands were locked from the beginning in an interservice rivalry that almost got out of hand. Jack says the Navy would get on the radio to complain that the Army was straying from formation, and then the Army would take the air to issue denials and a few charges of its own. If the Russians had attacked, they would not have had to fire a shot; the PBRs and the LCUs would have taken each other out.

Lieutenant John Carroll of the Coast Guard was asked to arbitrate. He was on Jack's boat for the day, and he represented the only other uniformed officer on the river. He says Commander Paul Schmella of the Navy argued initially that Lieutenant Gregg Smith of the Army was getting in the way, and he suggested a short while later that the Army be "ordered to the rear." Finally, the commander really got mad, and asked the

Coast Guard to "either force the LCUs out of formation or arrest the commanding officer of the Army vessels."

Lieutenant Carroll wondered if the next move would be a warning shot over the bow. "Never give 'em more than one barr'l to start with," as the Canadian journalist John Dafoe once said in a similar context, "but if they are foolish enough to ask for more, then give 'em the other barr'l right between the eyes." Worried that the armed forces might begin to bang each other up, for enlightenment, Lieutenant Carroll gave the microphone to Jack. "Come on guys," the fisherman said, "let's get on with the mission." Mercifully, they did.

That wasn't the only argument going on in the flotilla. Diana Reiss was having words with the federal government. She says the operation had been moving for several hours, the whale had been lured to the Pittsburg area, heading briskly to the Carquinez Strait, and suddenly: "We got a call from Charlie Fullerton. He was at the command center with the rest of the administrators, and he wanted to just stop everything in its tracks, so he could send someone out to try to stick another radio transmitter on the whale."

Dr. Reiss says she tried to stay calm, but the proposal was absurd. The fisheries agency had already tried to tag the animal four times, over more than a week, and failed utterly. Now the regional director wanted to stop a direct march to the sea for a fifth go-around. Debbie Ferrari complained to Jim Lecky that the government was more interested in tagging the animal than saving it, that it was endangering the entire operation for a whim, but Fullerton said that he would not be contradicted. His words reached all across the delta, but his thoughts were a few inches long.

"You can't do it, Charlie," Reiss said.

"Yes I can, " he replied.

"If you do, then I'm getting off this boat."

"Don't threaten me, Diana."

"I am threatening you. I know what I'm doing. I'm not going to stay out here and let you screw up the whole rescue."

Peigin Barrett was with Fullerton at command. She says the white-haired executive looked annoyed, but he relented. Dr. Reiss says she was angry for the rest of the afternoon, but relented when she appeared with Fullerton at a press conference. "Charlie introduced me. He said, 'This is a woman who stands up for what she believes. I said I was going to do one thing during the day, but she convinced me that I was wrong.' It was nice of him and, I might add, true."

When the whale swam past Benecia in the Carquinez Strait, thousands of people grouped on the shore for a look. Some of them stood at a vantage point that was under a railroad trestle. The Amtrak train was supposed to pass at the time, but it stopped short of the bridge for reasons of safety. Amtrak considered having police clear the area, but thought better of it. All those potential customers would have been inconvenienced, nay seething, and that's no way to run a railroad.

The Army LSUs pulled out of the operation at Carquinez Strait, but not, perish the thought, because of naval urging. Lieutenant Gregg Smith says he was not authorized to go any farther, although he admits that he was sorely tempted: "I didn't want to stop, and neither did my men. We felt that we had done our job very well, and we hated like hell to have to anchor our boats and let the [expletive deleted] Navy take over.

"I thought about my alternatives. I considered going on with the fleet anyway. I didn't want to disobey orders, but I felt I might get by with it if I called the rest of the trip a training mission. We wouldn't take part, you see, we would just follow the fleet and watch. It was a thought anyway. As it was, we just went home. We were pleased with what we'd done for the whale, but we weren't smiling."

Happiness, then, is not always a laughing matter. Everyone on the rescue mission was tickled to be moving Humphrey closer and closer to the ocean, but it was serious play. Jack says Senator Garamendi was so intent on success in this last attempt that he got on a boat for the first time, leaving the media to others, and banged a pipe from the San Joaquin River to San Pablo Bay. Jim Lecky, another desk jockey, also served in Findleton's crew.

"It all went remarkably well," Jack observes. "I'm not sure the tape recordings were entirely responsible, I think the boat formation and the pipe banging also served their purpose again. At any rate, the whale cooperated beautifully. Maybe he realized that this was it. Maybe he finally knew he was on his way home. He didn't stop once. He didn't try to turn around and mess everything up. He kept going in a relatively straight line toward San Francisco Bay."

The trip took all day and part of the night. It covered more than forty miles, and one of the troopers said it felt as if she had gone into another latitude. In fact, she did go into another latitude. The thirty-eighth parallel runs across the bottom of San Pablo Bay. It's the same demarcation that divides North and South Korea, roughly, and connects Athens, Greece, to Evansville, Indiana. The whale crossed the line well after dark, however, so it wasn't really visible.

Jack says that the trip was not only much smoother, it was much longer than expected. The original intention was to push Humphrey through the Carquinez Strait and leave him at the entrance to San Pablo Bay. The thinking was he could find his own way to the Pacific from there. The thinking changed with the heady success of the drive, however, and everyone agreed that the boats should continue to move the Mysticeti right to the Golden Gate and into the sea itself.

Thus, there would be another day's working. Humphrey was lured under the Richmond—San Rafael Bridge at about 10:00 P.M. That's the span that separates San Pablo from San Francisco Bay, and the boat crews lost sight of him in the dark near the Tiburon Peninsula of Marin County. The whale swam back to the east side of the bridge, by the lights at the Richmond Long Pier. Everyone crossed his fingers and shared the hope that the good old boy would stay put and go to sleep.

The seeds of still another rescue dispute were planted that night on the shore. Bernie Krause, the audiologist who didn't think the tape recordings would work, changed his mind substantially. He told the news media that luring the whale with the sounds of other whales was an impressive scientific achievement, and whether by design or reporting error, he gained a good lot of personal credit.

That infuriated the man who had provided the tapes, Dr. Lou Herman of the University of Hawaii. He says the tapes were the property of his students, and he had the idea for their use; yet "here was this other joker" elbowing in on the glory. Herman says the university's marine mammal program should have received "the full attribution," but it ended up as if it hadn't done anything at all:

"Bernie Krause did not even want to play the recordings at first. He said it wasn't worth the effort. Then when it was clear that a breakthrough had been made, he stood up to take the bows. It's scientific thievery. We did not get any credit, except in the Hawaii newspapers. We sent the tapes in good faith, and that man got the publicity and honor."

Bill Clemmensen owns a marine repair business in Sacramento. He also captained a repair boat for Operation Whale rescue. When the last day's mission began on November 4, he was asked to look at a faulty alternator on one of the vessels. When he drove to the rendezvous, he was unexpectedly rewarded. He got the first look at the whale that morning. He also got the first and only recorded sight of Humphrey breaching, jumping all the way out of the water like a trout for a fly.

Clemmensen says it was tumultuous, and he is not a man who wastes superlatives. He says the whale was swimming ninety to one hundred feet from the Richmond Bridge on the San Pablo side, and it was apparently playing. It swam in small circles, then leaped out of the water, twisting a little before it dropped in a crashing belly flop. Clemmensen says the whale breached many times, and he thinks it may have been part of a feeding gambit or maybe he was just refreshed. After twenty-five days, the animal was finally back in salt water.

The last day's operation team was worried by some early A.M. discombobulations. Jack says there were mechanical difficulties with the tape-recorder boat, *Bootlegger,* and after that, the biologists decided that the whale was in what they called a "rest pattern," and should not be immediately pestered:

So we blew the best part of the day. It had started out with calm winds and good water, but, as the morning wore on, the weather changed. The wind picked up, there was a chop in the bay, and I was very concerned about fog that was settling over the Golden Gate Bridge. It looked like a storm.

I got nervous, and the Coast Guard got nervous. When Debbie asked if we could wait for one more hour, I said the maximum was fifteen minutes. Even that was too long. By the time we were underway, the waves were two feet or more, and the wind was stiff. I got the boats in formation, however, and Bootlegger got out in front. The plan was to guide the whale down through Raccoon Strait, which runs between the Tiburon Peninsula and Angel Island. That was the most direct route to the Pacific Ocean, which was still eight to ten miles away over increasingly agitated water.

The water was so bad, actually, I think it interfered with the playing of the feeding tapes, because when the sound was turned on, Humphrey did not respond. Bernie Krause and Diana Reiss monkeyed with the sound level, and Jim Cook drove the boat all around the whale, but nothing happened, zilch. The winds were blowing, the water was rolling, and I don't think Humphrey could hear the tapes in the commotion. It was a lousy beginning. The whale would not go toward Raccoon Strait. Instead, he swam over to the Southhampton Shoals, where he pointed toward Treasure Island.

John Carroll of the Coast Guard was still on my boat. We were getting more and more leery of the weather, so I decided that someone had to make a move. Sometimes it's better to do something, and apologize later, than to wait forever for permission. I told John I was changing the plan. He agreed it was the best thing to do. I dropped Bootlegger, dropped the tape recordings, and dropped Raccoon Strait. I began to push Humphrey the same way as in Shag Slough, with the pipe-banging boats alone, and we went in the direction he seemed to prefer, toward the city of San Francisco.

Rio Vista was now fifty miles away from the action, but the residents were not going to forget a visitor that had made such large deposits in their economic and psychological accounts. A gravestone artisan named John ("The Chisler") Silva donated a stone for Humphrey monument, which would be placed at the foot of Main Street, near the water, and a junior high school student named Richard Fonbuena wrote the inscription:

> Humphrey the humpback whale,
>   A mighty whale was he,
> He swam into the delta,
>   To see what he could see.

There's more, but forget it. Diana Del-Zampo of the Chamber of Commerce says it's the thought that counts. The thought is permanent sentiment, of course, and increased tourism.

The Coast Guard notified the rescue boats that a nuclear submarine had come through the Golden Gate and was moving upwater on the bay, toward the Concord Naval Weapons Station. Barry Canevero says the whole thing was positively strange. The whale was on one side; the submarine was on the other, the natural order as opposed to the technological state, saving lives here and taking them there. It gave one pause.

The moment was at hand. Time had flown and carried the events with it admirably. Jack had reduced the size of his flotilla to eighteen maneuverable boats. He had pushed the whale to deep water below Southhampton Shoals, and he notified his command that the whale had, by mid-afternoon, picked up speed dramatically:

He was flat out. He had been doing two or three knots at Red Rock near the bridge. Now he was up to six knots or seven, and this was in three-foot waves. I had lost the trim tabs [stabilizing flaps] on the boat, and I was bouncing around like a rubber duck in a fat lady's bath.

John Carroll came to the rescue. He could see that I was trying to drive the boat, maintain the formation, and keep radio control with hand-held devices, so he said he would take the wheel. That left me free to concentrate solely on the drive. I went to the stern of the boat, with a pair of portable radios, and I gave orders and directions from there. Actually, it was the best seat in the universe then. Everything had fallen into place. Humphrey had stopped playing around, and he certainly wasn't in a "rest pattern" anymore. He was on his way to find mom and dad.

I only had two problems that I could see, and one could be readily handled. Jim Cook in Bootlegger was acting up. When they shut off the tape recordings on his boat, he was no longer leading the pack, and he was not as responsible as he should have been. He kept getting on the radio with useless things, tying up the air time. He said he had the whale off his beam, when he wasn't anywhere near the animal. I finally had to remind him that there was only one fellow in command of the mission. I was it, and we were too close to the end of the operation to argue about it.

He straightened out then, and that left the second problem.

Humphrey was heading to the west of Treasure Island, which was fine, but I was worried that he might slip down around the island, then between it and San Francisco, and wind up in the vicinity of the Oakland Bay Bridge. If he did that, he could go on into the lower part of San Francisco Bay, a place where there is a preponderance of shallow water. The last thing in the world we wanted was to strand the thing on the mud flats of Alameda or in the bogs of San Mateo, where millions of people could come out to watch him die.

Barry and I had discussed the possibility. That's why we never tried to block the bridge with boats. We knew that, all through the operation, as far back as Liberty Island, Humphrey tended to take a right turn when he came to a bridge, and, by God, that's what he did again. When he got to the point where he had to make a decision at San Francisco, he turned right. That's when I felt we had finally won the contest. I lined the Navy boats out from the shore. I used San Francisco as a block on the other side, and all we did then was push Humphrey though that lane toward the Golden Gate.

"What a thing that was, and the whale played it to the hilt. There were tens of thousands of people lining the Embarcadero, and more arriving by the minute. The workday was ending. People were coming out of their offices for the show. I remember that Charlie Fullerton was so excited he got to thinking about the media implications. He called someone to ask us if we could get the whale under the Golden Gate Bridge by the five o'clock news. John Carroll looked at me, and we rolled our eyes. Then he sent a return message saying that, if Charlie will lift the fog, that's a roger.

As it turned out, we did it with time to spare. We got to the bridge just about the time rush hour was starting. Barry was out in front, on my starboard bow, I was off his port stern. We drove Humphrey toward the south tower of the bridge. Barry then got on the phone and said, 'Hey, remember our promise, you better get up here.' John Carroll asked what he meant, and I told him that we had a pact that we were going to drive the whale through the bridge side by side. I told John the pact now included him, because, as far as I was concerned, the three of us deserved it.

I pulled up. It was a hell of a scene. The people were screaming on the shore. The foghorns were loud in the soup. There were helicopters overhead, people at the rail of the bridge, traffic slowing down to a crawl, boats giving us the right-of-way—and then I saw Humphrey's tail on the other side of the bridge. I yelled it out like a schoolboy. "He's through, he's through." I waved at Barry in his boat, I slapped John Carroll on the backside. Then, I, suppose, I cried. I admit it, I bawled. It was one of the best moments of my life."

Hal Alabaster of NOAA announced that Humphrey had swum out of the bay at 4:30 P.M. Debbie Ferrari said it was like a rebirth. A spectator named Mary Roberts said God was a member of the rescue crew, and Peigin Barrett said nothing would ever be impossible again. Jack followed the whale past the Colregs Demarkation line, which is the official start of the Pacific Ocean. The last time he saw the creature, it was rolling west in high seas, off Seal Rock, two miles from the bridge, two weeks from Shag Slough, home at long last.

epilogue

THE WHALE LEFT THE SACRAMENTO RIVER DELTA IN APparent good health, though the inland journey could not have done him any good, and judging from the history of the species, it probably went to winter grounds off the Baja Peninsula or Hawaii. Debbie and Mark Ferrari say the animal is quite easily identifiable and will be known if it makes another appearance.

Meanwhile, science continues to wonder why the animal got lost. The truth is that we never found out very much about his thinking or his motivations. We did find out once again that the measure of a fine deed is that it seems inevitable in retrospect, and we most certainly learned a little more about ourselves during this thoroughly American folk epic.

About the Authors

Jack Findleton, 37, was a member of the elite 101st Airborne Division in Vietnam. Today he captains his own fishing boat in the Sacramento River. This is his first book.

Tom Tiede, 48, is an award-winning journalist and author of five books, including two novels, *Coward* and *Welcome to Washington, Mr. Witherspoon.* Tiede is one of America's most widely published feature writers and in the past 20 years he has traveled more than one and a half million miles in search of stories, which he has filed from 68 countries and every one of the 50 states. He has received many distinguished national journalism awards, including The Ernie Pyle Award for outstanding feature writing.

Pharos Books are available at special discounts on bulk purchases for sales promotions, premiums, fundraising or educational use. For details, contact the Special Sales Department, Pharos Books, 200 Park Avenue, New York, NY 10166.

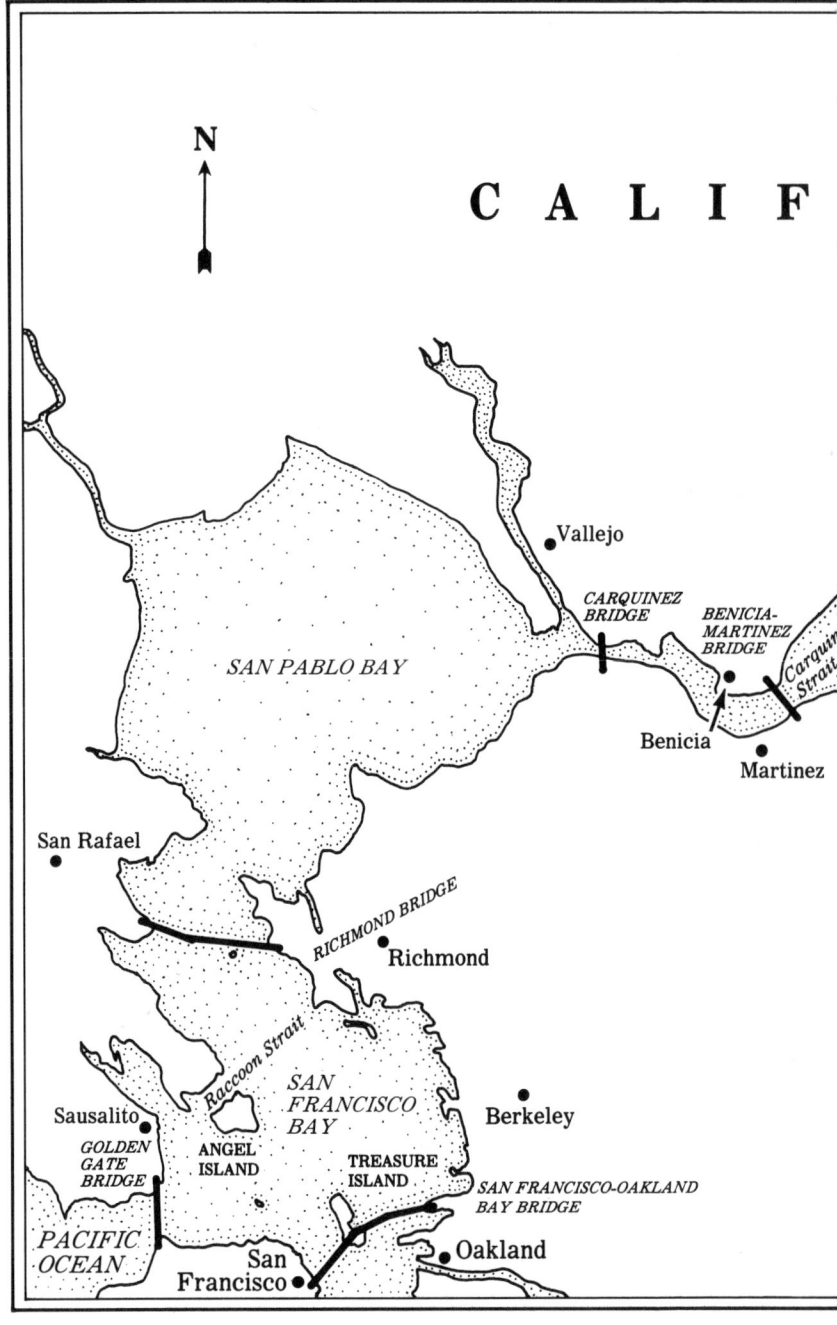